Praise for *The Earthquake*

"Life has its ups and downs; however, we should never give up hope. There is a saying in Tibetan; 'Persevere even if you fail nine times.' Vince Poscente's book, *The Earthquake*, will inspire many to meet the difficult challenges of life."

—Dalai Lama

"After surviving a catastrophic plane crash in the Andes and 72-days of refusing to die, I learned a great deal about friendship, tragedy, and perseverance. *The Earthquake* is more than a story about a personal 'earthquake.' It is a formula to escape the feeling of being stuck and into the light of hope."

—Nando Parrado, leader of the *Miracle in the Andes* and featured in the film *Alive*

"Living through a genocide, not having food, water, electricity, medicine, or outside contact. Getting severely injured by a rocket propelled grenade (RPG), having my leg amputated without anesthesia, having over 100 surgeries, having to re-learn how to walk, taking 15 years to learn how to run has landed me in many predicaments, created many setbacks and 'earthquakes' that I had to master. One of the toughest of all was mastering my 'elephant' and building the relationship between my elephant and my ant. I can only wish I had this book to help guide me from seemingly impossible situations to breakthroughs! If you want to take your life to the next level, and master life to not only survive, but thrive, read this book because Vince has done the hard work for us and outlined the lessons in a very practical, clever, and entertaining way. Love it!"

—Maja Kazazic, Bosnian genocide survivor and Vela Business Solutions founder

"Your 'earthquake' may have only happened once, but it can indeed live rent-free in your brain until you find your way out of the setback you experienced. Learn from *The Earthquake* to escape the insidious nature of fear and limiting beliefs."

—Steven Pressfield, international bestselling author of *The War of Art*

"Polarization is the enemy. Alignment is the path to peace. No matter the scale of the setbacks you experience, you can find a way past the struggles that come from limiting beliefs. Read and learn from *The*

Earthquake to truly supersede any obstacles you experience in your life."

"It is in that still and lonely place that we learn life's most transformative lessons. *The Earthquake* is a how-to guide for anyone who's ever hit rock bottom and sees no way up. It is about triumph in the midst of tragedy, of overcoming the seemingly insurmountable, and it is about an inexhaustible faith under fire."

"What goes on inside our head controls what goes on outside of it, especially when we experience any setback or, even, devastation. Read *The Earthquake* to get unstuck and thrive in your life."

"In the business of life, we each, eventually, face a life altering setback or personal devastation. How you respond can be the difference between feeling stuck or breaking through. Read *The Earthquake* to break free."

"Life is a daring adventure. Inevitably, adversity will meet you. But you'll likely remain stuck until you choose to overcome it. Fear will rise. This is an invitation to be courageous. For years, Vince has been an inspiration for me. I can vouch for the integrity that laces every word in this engaging, practical, and entertaining book. Read it!"

"From managing the top entertainment talent in the world to personal setbacks that brought me to my knees, I completely identified with the value in this book. Here's to your own breakthroughs."

"As a fellow former athlete who found a way to translate experiences in the arena toward lifelong growth and service, Vince shares the same passion in helping people be free from their setbacks. Reading this book will empower you to escape the familiarity of a setback and be free to choose the future within your reach."

—Lance Allred, first deaf player in NBA
history and inspirational speaker

"The integrative/functional medicine approach to treating and preventing cancer is my life's work. You treat the chaos that can happen with personal earthquakes for those you love. This is a great guidebook to treating the chaos."

—Leigh Erin Connealy, MD, author of *Be Perfectly
Healthy* and *The Cancer Revolution*

"If you haven't experienced the devastation of your own personal 'earthquake,' chances are you will. Learn from the Ant and Elephant's story of friendship, tragedy, and perseverance and use it to appreciate the gift of life and the instinct to thrive that exists in all of us."

—Aron Ralston, depicted in the film *127 Hours* and *New York
Times* bestselling author of *Between a Rock and a Hard Place*

The Earthquake

Also by Vince Poscente

The Ant and the Elephant: Leadership for the Self
The Age of Speed: Learning to Thrive in a More-Faster-Now World
Heroes Climb: The Ascent from I to Us
Silver Bullets: 75 Straightforward Tips to Take You to the Top
Invinceable Principles: Essential Tools for Life Mastery

The
Earthquake

YOUR JOURNEY FROM SETBACK TO BREAKTHROUGH

Vince Poscente

Matt Holt Books
An Imprint of BenBella Books, Inc.
Dallas, TX

Matt Holt Books is an imprint of BenBella Books, Inc.
10440 N. Central Expressway
Suite 800
Dallas, TX 75231
benbellabooks.com
Send feedback to feedback@benbellabooks.com

BenBella is a federally registered trademark. MATT HOLT and logo are trademarks of BenBella Books.

Printed in the United States of America
10 9 8 7 6 5 4 3 2 1

Library of Congress Control Number: 2021026218
ISBN 9781953295712 (trade cloth)
ISBN 9781637740057 (ebook)

Editing by Katie Dickman and Alyn Wallace
Copyediting by Michael Fedison
Proofreading by Karen O'Brien and Sarah Vostok
Text design and composition by PerfecType, Nashville, TN
Cover design by Brigid Pearson
Cover images © Shutterstock shaineast (savannah), noeldelmar (fault line),
    NadzeyaShanchuk (ant), Benguhan (elephant)
Map illustration by Simona Molino
Plumeria illustration by Varsha U
Printed by Lake Book Manufacturing

Special discounts for bulk sales are available. Please contact bulkorders@benbellabooks.com.

Dedicated to Michelle, Max, Alexia, and Isabella

Contents

Map

Hint: Start at the Oasis

Character Key

Adir the Ant—our hero as a metaphor for the conscious mind who's inextricably connected to his habit-driven elephant, Elgo

Elgo the Elephant—the powerful subconscious mind who ultimately dictates where Adir will end up

Brio the Owl—teacher/mentor who provides timely guidance for Adir and Elgo

Chromia the Wolf—the villain who makes life worse for Adir and Elgo

Valafar the Vulture—a scoundrel who demonstrates the contradiction concept

Aria—a spunky, confident ant who befriends Adir and Elgo

Ella—Aria's elephantine subconscious character rescuer in dark times

Author's Note

Our Journey from Setback to Breakthrough

There's **no** linear way
out of **chaos**.

B ack in 1992, I heard Dr. Lee Pulos, a clinical psychologist on the faculty of the University of British Columbia Medical School and sports psychologist for the Canadian Olympic team and the Edmonton Oilers, explain: "Based on scientific research, in one second of time, the conscious mind utilizes two thousand neurons. In the same second, your subconscious mind ('sub' meaning below, 'conscious' meaning awareness) utilizes four *billion* neurons."

Sit on that statistic for a moment.

Your conscious mind is whirring away with two thousand neurons, each housed in the glial cells of your brain, zipping back and forth, to and fro, in a complex pattern producing conscious thought. You are reading these words. At the same time, you may be distracted by the sound of your teenager playing a video game in the other room. Or you remember your dry cleaning needs to be picked up.

One thought after another.

You have a profound awareness every second of your waking life, all because of two thousand neurons at work in your conscious mind.

Now imagine the power of the four billion neurons firing off in your subconscious.

It's a ratio of activity that's roughly equivalent to the size difference between an ant and the largest land animal on Earth: the elephant.* So if your conscious mind is an ant and your subconscious mind is an elephant, who is more likely to have control? If an ant fought an elephant, who would win?

Have you ever decided one thing, but ended up in a completely different place? You consciously decide to go on a diet. Two thousand neurons, every second, kick into gear. You strive to "make"

---

* The scientific community might scoff at a metaphor of conscious and subconscious "thought" identical to the ratio of an ant and an elephant, but set your ant-mind aside and stick with me.

it happen. But if "I don't think so. I refuse to go on a diet!" is the subconscious decision all along, you'll never lose the weight.

But what if your conscious and your subconscious were on the exact same page?

What if every one of your two thousand conscious neuronal intentions and all four billion susceptible, subconscious neurons pointed in the exact same direction? How powerful would you be with that kind of alignment? How much easier would life become? How many obstacles in life would you blow right by?

In the prequel to this book, *The Ant and the Elephant*, I explored exactly those questions. It was a parable about an ant realizing he is on the back of an elephant. They are inextricably linked. They go everywhere together. Where they end up, they are, of course, together. Imagine the ant, Adir, decides, "I want to go west." He starts marching west.

But what if Elgo the Elephant is headed east? Which way is Adir really going?

East.

All while believing that he is, in fact, going west.

At first, does the ant see an elephant under him? No. Adir can only observe "the ground" as a grey landscape with tall, skinny trees (elephant hairs) to navigate past. The ant eventually realizes his goal of going west to reach an oasis will never happen until he convinces his elephant to turn west and go to the oasis, too.

In *The Ant and the Elephant*, I explored the many aspects that may have kept *your* ant and elephant from aligning. There are limiting beliefs, negative patterns, bad habits, childhood wounds, early trauma, and all sorts of psychological speed bumps that counselors and psychologists make their well-earned living from. People have relationship issues, self-confidence setbacks, self-esteem struggles, and other areas where they seek personal or professional clarity. My original parable simplified a way to find clarity for its readers. I also addressed any discord that can happen between conscious thought and limiting subconscious patterns and habits. I offered tools to align your conscious ant decisions with your powerful, subconscious elephant. In the prequel, we learned how to reach that oasis—to get your ant and elephant on the same page and find paradise.

But what happens when your world is rocked by some sort of setback or profoundly limiting event? The kind that dramatically ruptures the relationship between the conscious and subconscious mind? An event so drastic that I'll call it an earthquake. What happens when you, at best, have lost your footing but, at worst, have lost everything? What then? The tools Adir used to steer Elgo to the "oasis" won't work as they did in the past. That oasis doesn't even *exist* anymore.

I know they won't work because years after I wrote *The Ant and the Elephant*, I had my own personal earthquake.

Just before the Great Recession, I was riding high. Not only was I one of the youngest National Speakers Association Hall of Fame speakers joining the likes of Ronald Reagan, Og Mandino, Zig Ziglar, and Jim Rohn, but I was inducted into Canada's

Speaker Hall of Fame, had a *New York Times* bestselling book, and commanded more for a one-hour speech than I made in an entire year in my job after college. My speaking calendar was full. I never took any of it for granted. I was truly fortunate. I knew it and was grateful almost every waking moment.

I was also ambitious. What was next on this rocket ship ride?

My wife and I built our dream home. My future speeches would have certainly paid for it—except that, at the same time, I invested in a project that rivaled the cost of our home. I tied up the money that I needed to pay for the new home into that other project. I thought this highly exposed, risky move was a wise investment because the projections were promising indeed. But then the economy crashed and most of my speaking bookings canceled.

From the outside, the optics of our life were: *the Poscentes are wealthy.* The new home, massive property, upscale neighborhood—it appeared as if we were riding high. But we weren't. We were broke.

Within months, I was being squashed under crushing debt. My wife and I made our skinny list. Somehow, we stayed in our dream home, but everything else had to go. We stopped going on holidays to faraway lands. I became the yard guy, the pool boy, and made just enough to maintain my fifteen-year-old car. For family meals, we would have lentils and salad. When the water got cut off, I would juggle finances yet again. I didn't know where the next paycheck would come from. With my calendar empty, I would sit at my desk, my head in my hands, crying, because I felt like I had let everyone down.

The Great Recession, combined with my faltering ambition, left me confused, disoriented, and on a downward trajectory. It was a hole that was impossible to climb out of. Our debt was massive and overwhelming. Collectors would call, then harass, then threaten the worst. I was sued and forced into multiple depositions. "Where's our money and why won't you pay?" There was a five-city business trip where I left home with $70 to last the entire week. I had no credit cards (they were taken away long ago) and no safety net (everyone I borrowed money from was tapped out). Our lifestyle completely changed from abundance to scarcity.

The debt-collecting wolves closed in and the opportunistic vultures circled overhead. We learned quickly who our friends were and who trod on us from their high horse.

Our personal earthquake happened and I didn't know how to reinvent and keep climbing. I falsely assumed, "I made it to the Olympics and built business success! Of course I'll be able to get out of this mess!" I repeatedly assumed the formula I used to go from weekend skier to an Olympic athlete in four years, this same prescriptive formula that brought me to an award-winning speaking career, #1 on the *Wall Street Journal* bestselling list, the very same linear, step-by-step formula that is in *The Ant and the Elephant* would be the formula to escape my financial devastation. Instead, everything I tried sputtered or barely produced revenue. I fought our financial mess. I pushed to sell my way out of the pervasive setback. I tried forcing new revenue-generating ideas and nearly gave up, while feeling impossibly stuck. I did not yet realize there is no linear way out of chaos. I felt helpless.

This "stuckness" came from the growing fissure with the most personal relationship anyone can ever have: the relationship within myself—between my ant and my elephant. When we have an earthquake, our conscious mind frantically searches for solutions that have served it well in the past, without accepting that this is no longer the past. This is a new reality. When we are so focused on a way out, we often forget how much the aftershocks of a trauma plus our own unwillingness to consider new outcomes are weighing down our subconscious. It is when there is that discord between your own *ant* and *elephant* that you will remain in the state of *stuckness*.

What brought us out of the hole is the Solution Loop that unfolds in the pages of this book. In a fashion, this book is a map of the path out of any earthquake you may experience in your life. It's not a shortcut—there is no shortcut. But there is a way to escape stuckness and find the solution that will help you on your way to a new oasis of freedom. The tools that I discovered to get myself and my family out of that stuckness are what you will read about in this book. These are tools that I've found made me more than happy—I feel fulfilled.

Is there another earthquake coming?

Of course. No oasis is permanent, and the human condition is complex. Some kind of personal earthquake undoubtedly awaits us. But it is when discomfort pushes us back out into the desert that we can learn to become our most creative selves and uncover, or stumble upon, previously hidden solutions.

The Earthquake is a new parable that uncovers that very non-linear process. In this story, you will discover how to transform the setbacks that knock your professional goals off track or keep you spinning in place for years into profound breakthroughs. You will journey from frustrating obstacles to an alignment of your intentions and actions. You will discover your very own Solution Loop. Therein, may this book lead you from darkness to light, to your new Oasis.

CHAPTER I

Accepting a New Reality

J ust before sunrise, a swelling wave of sound washed over the dense and rolling carpet of treetops. One bird braved the silence, quickly followed by two, then four, then eight, sounding as a new day's wake-up call. Soon, thousands ushered in the gradual light that turns darkness into shades of color. Vibrant greens and blues were complemented by shadows retreating into the undulating contours of the land.

Adir the Ant's favorite time to slip from dreamland into another serene early morning began to unfold. He opened one eye, then the other, took a deep breath, and stretched all six legs. Rolling to a sitting position on the back of his elephant, then standing up, he threw his gaze across the Oasis in front of him. The elephant, Elgo, underneath him was also slowly rousing.

Adir closed his eyes and took another deep breath. He felt gratitude wash over him for the journey that brought him to this magical valley.

Adir's trek to the Oasis was no minor feat. Just a decade ago he didn't even know that he was inextricably linked to an elephant. Despite his intention to find the mythical Oasis, he'd never be able to reach it if his elephant, Elgo, did not also want to take the same journey to an unknown land.

Ten years ago, Adir learned valuable lessons from Brio, a sage mentor and respected owl across the Savannah. Brio was the first to explain how Adir, like other special ants, was on the back of a special elephant. Ants have instincts, thoughts, and intentions, but it was the powerful Elgo, Adir's elephant, who could direct Adir's actions with his own instincts, patterns, and agenda that either aligned, or didn't, with the directions Adir intended to go.

Before knowing he was on the back of an elephant, Adir had gotten word that the Oasis of his dreams was west. As one does when a goal takes hold, Adir started marching west. Yet, the more he drove forward with his signature willpower, the more it sunk in that he was ending up east. "How can this be?" he bellowed to the heavens.

Brio heard Adir's desperate call and took pity on him, proceeding to teach Adir how to align one's antlike intentions with the elephantine drivers below Adir's six determined feet.

It took time for Adir to understand Brio's lessons, but he had to. Aligning with his pachyderm Elgo was essential before he could reach the Oasis. Thus began the ant and the elephant's journey of self-discovery.

Still with his eyes closed, and taking another deep breath, he reflected on how vital it was to have clarity of vision in order to reach the Oasis. Only by fixating on the emotion of arriving at the Oasis was it possible to get Elgo on board for a march west. Adir thought about the power of commitment as it related to their consistent efforts. He used Gold Dots as an emotional trigger to remind himself of his dream destination. His Gold Dots were a reminder to imagine the five senses associated with his Oasis. Each time he imagined the sights, sounds, tastes, textures, and smells of his future home, combined with the satisfaction, joy, and fulfillment that he'd feel once he reached his goal, Adir would feel a buzz up and down his spine while his elephant would shudder in delight. It always amazed him how this powerful "elephant buzz" would keep him on track.

High atop his elephant's back, Adir looked around the valley and reminisced about how they had met with obstacles that stood in their way. He chuckled when he remembered how petrified Elgo could become when confronting the tiniest of fears, like a mischievous mouse, while having the bravery to take on a powerful pride of lions. Adir smiled, as he often did, when he thought of the techniques he'd used to redirect Elgo's attention. Distractions and the derailing of their journey by Elgo's relatives Nega and Holic had disrupted their progress. To get back on track, Adir redirected his, and the elephant's attention toward a Gold Dot, which again triggered the elephant buzz of living in the Oasis.

Adir remembered the weeks and months of frustration that allowed hopelessness to take root, when negativity from the outside was coupled with pessimism from within. Now, though, remembering it gave Adir confidence in his ability to overcome any despair with the life-changing technique of having a conversation with his elephant by first asking, "Is this gloomy thought taking us closer to our elephant buzz or further away?" If the answer was, "Further away," then Adir knew to clearly state, "Thank you, Elgo, but that's not part of our vision. Our vision is a life at the amazingly wonderful Oasis." As Adir reflected on that technique he'd used to build confidence, he was brought back to the five senses and emotion.

There it was again.

The scintillating elephant buzz underneath his feet. While both Adir and Elgo looked out at the actual Oasis, they experienced the visceral vibration that came from being aligned in pursuit of their goal. There was simply no better feeling. They were totally in sync and aligned in every way.

Adir thought about the routines they had used to get and stay on course. With his dynamic imagination, Adir remembered how he created a stack of flash cards to prepare himself for any stressful scenario they may encounter in the future. Over the course of days and weeks, Adir would join his elephant in imagining how well they would handle any challenge or obstacle. That simple technique had brought them, ultimately, to a fulfilling arrival in the Oasis.

Adir grinned at the memory of the gratitude he'd felt on the midnight of their arrival. As he and Elgo trundled over the rise to see a valley before them, instantaneous peace of mind had washed over him. The stars had reflected in the water below, dancing with delight on their arrival. It was a journey filled with challenges and uncertainties, but they'd made it. Step by step across the Savannah, they'd made their dream come true.

Adir's gratitude enveloped him and Elgo yet again.

He felt another shudder under his feet—but this sensation sent dread down his back, morphing into something ominous and unsettling. In an instant, the forest of birds went completely quiet. Elgo suddenly shifted and Adir lost his balance—something that hadn't happened since he'd learned about Elgo—and had to catch himself.

His eyes shot open to see the sky full of birds dashing in all directions in an instinctive surge of survival. It happened again. First a jerk, then a wobble.

"EARTHQUAKE!" he heard someone yell. "The kids. Get the kids! Run to open space. RUN!"

Thick, wet dust clung to the air. The ground shuddered again. Deep subsonic sounds rumbled in the distance as horror set in.

Adir and, underneath his feet, his silent pachyderm partner, Elgo, couldn't believe their eyes. Nothing seemed real. Adir caught a glimpse of the Oasis pond undulating, then vanishing into nothingness. A sickening crack in the earth decimated their Oasis.

As Adir clung on to Elgo's neck, he gradually got a full picture of the massive extent of the destruction. Ruptures in the earth spewed air and dirt, while the world around them tried to adapt to seismic shifts in the terrain.

Everything they knew was gone, and nothing would be the same.

Adir couldn't comprehend what had happened to his surroundings. The devastation was too massive. His brain continuously rang a bell of denial, repeating, "How could this happen? The spring-fed pond can't just disappear. Nothing bad happens in the Oasis. This can't happen to us."

The more "How could this happen?" rang in his head, the more off balance he felt.

The refrain repeated for a day, as pods of wildlife left the Oasis in a steady, frothing stream. The fearful animals grabbed their belongings and valuables and left the wreckage, heading east for a faraway port city.

Adir and Elgo's friends were safe. Adir didn't even notice until later in the day that all the children were completely oblivious to the carnage, their tiny voices and laughter echoing around the newly formed rocky terrain.

The kids had no sense of loss, Adir realized, because loss has to do with fear—particularly of an unknown future. Concerned only about their game of tag, the kids had no concerns about what lay ahead. Now was all that mattered.

Adir wished he were a kid, too.

A small dark cloud tried to sneak into Adir's thoughts but, as was his habit, he focused instead on what he knew to be true: a glass is always on its way to being full, never empty. He would be an eternal optimist. Repeating his mantra—"I'll figure it out"—made him instantly feel better.

While Adir was cleaning up and repairing what he could, he returned to business. The folks he worked with were also all unnerved by the earthquake. Who wouldn't be? But this catastrophic event felt different than other setbacks or obstacles he had experienced in the past. A devastation of this proportion was life-changing in a confusing way. Uncertainty was the only thing he was certain of. He tried to get his work-life back to normal, but nothing was normal. Customers simply canceled their contracts. Not one, but a handful, walked away from their deposit and simply turned their back on their agreement, too shaken to care.

Adir had been here before. He scanned back to earlier times when his business was booming. With the *Wall Creek Journal* reporting record profits across all Oasis industry, Adir and Elgo decided it was time for a bold move. While building their dream house, a home that would house Adir and Elgo on a luxurious estate, they also pushed for a Savannah-wide consulting practice like no other. They knew in their bones the risk was worth taking. Winners are courageous. They are bold. They take challenges head-on.

Adir kept writing checks. "You've got to spend money to make money." Adir knew the leverage landscape, too. He had leveraged money in real estate on the other side of the Oasis. He made a tidy sum turning a few thousand dollars into tens of thousands with a few rental properties.

This time, the stakes were higher. He knew his opportunity was huge. He also looked around and saw others who had grown large practices. Minimize the risk, leverage the cash, borrow high-interest money to leverage if you must, and take challenges head-on. It was an aggressive move, but the old proverb "Meek ants and elephants shall inherit the earth" was a saying he didn't buy into. "Go big or go home to your anthill" and "No temporary pain, no elephant-sized gain" were more his style.

While Adir and Elgo had been building their lives, Brio the Owl spent his time flying from one area to another mentoring creatures in need. He was known for his profound insights and measured advice. He would check in on his ant and elephant friends at times when he could. Brio marveled at Adir's ambition. He would reminisce on the early days when Adir started on his journey to the Oasis. He remembered how he taught Adir and Elgo how to be truly aligned. He felt good about his mentorship that helped the duo meet setbacks head-on. But now, the duo was filled with confidence. They didn't need help. They were on top of their world.

During an overnight visit in an Oasis stopover, Brio had popped in to visit his enterprising friends. The perceptive owl could tell the aggressive business plans Adir and Elgo were taking were risky. It reminded him of a rock avalanche he saw on the other side of the Western Mountains.

Brio loved to teach in metaphor. He chose his brief time with them to share a story. "Across the land, there was a deadly avalanche that occurred well before you both arrived here at the Oasis. On that sad day, a large outcropping of massive rocks had clung precariously to the apex of Saronja Mountain. As I was flying across the valley, one of the larger rocks caught my attention. At first, the loose boulder started to pick up speed and hit a few more boulders. Two boulders hit four, then eight, then chaos ensued. A massive landslide laid claim to everything in its path.

"Even if there had only been one rock careening down the mountain, the destruction would have been substantial, but with so many, the devastation was exponential, fanning out and burying the serenity that had existed down below. Every living thing at the base of the mountain was buried by the rocks that killed them."

Adir and Elgo sat across from their owl friend. They were unsure of Brio's message. The sage owl shuddered at the memory as he swiveled his head and refocused on the life in the Oasis that Adir and Elgo had built.

"You've both built a wonderful life here. Just be sure you aren't building it under a potential landslide of unseen peril," said Brio with an encouraging tone.

"Brio, we got this," said Adir. "Sometimes I think you worry too much."

Brio left it at that.

The next day, he continued to think about Adir and Elgo. It's hard to watch someone take themselves on a collision course toward destiny. "But what can I do?" he thought to himself. "Some just have to learn the hard way. Creatures just don't seem to change course until they experience some sort of massive setback." Resignation laced his voice as he hooted.

The feeling Brio had for his friends would foreshadow the earthquake they would soon experience. He could not fathom the decimation the worst natural disaster the Oasis would experience in a hundred years would cause—or what it would do to Adir and Elgo's partnership. Their business, home, and even their well-earned confidence would be literally shaken and destroyed. They would eventually realize they needed to find solutions that were not part of their typical relationship. Time would reveal their new path.

After the earthquake, Adir's frustration mounted. He tried countless times to convince his fellow creatures not to leave the Oasis. As more members of the community left, Elgo felt more and more anxious. Adir, meanwhile, continued to be optimistic. "We must stay. We must rebuild this broken ground. We can figure this out," he would plead to minds already made up. "Then Elgo and I will do this alone!" he would retort to unbending ears. Clients would either disappear or flat-out say, "Stop calling me." For month upon month, what seemed like feelings of intense hesitation from Elgo were met with a crescendo of abject frustration from Adir.

With grey skies above, and stillness in the air after a recent shower, Adir, on the back of Elgo, started to sob, relieved no one could see him. A new feeling crept into Adir's psyche. It was like tasting sour milk for the first time. But this libation was soured confidence. At first, he thought it was persistent doubt. But the more the uncertainty took hold, the less confident he felt. He simply could not process what had happened to his signature confidence. He could tell Elgo was shaken, too. He and Elgo were behind a collection of boulders and trees. No one could see them as Adir couldn't hold back the tears. He needed to pull himself together for his own well-being and as an inseparable partner to his easily influenced elephant.

But he couldn't stop sobbing because what he'd seen after he'd noticed the children playing hopscotch had sent him into a downward spiral. Adir poked his head over the edge of Elgo's brow. A recent rain had left puddles of water, like contorted reflections of what lay above. He could see carefree clouds meander across the sky. He thought of the children and their complete lack of concern for anything but the fun at hand. He stretched his neck out farther and saw his reflection in a puddle directly below. He looked into his own eyes. There was sad desperation he had not seen before. Then, almost as if it was the anti-elephant buzz, the opposite of a feeling of excitement overcame him. It was more of a sinking feeling, like a waterlogged piece of wood drifting downward into darker depths. This feeling matched a fragility in Elgo's constitution that he'd never felt before. He was not sure what that feeling was, but he abhorred the sensation as it infested his being.

Adir kept noticing how fragile he and his elephant felt. Never in his life had he felt anything like this. Adir's "rugged-individual mentality" consistently brought him achievements. While he knew he needed support from his powerful companion to get to any destination, he also knew how much willpower he had. Whenever he mastered his will, he achieved and succeeded at anything he set his mind to.

But this time was different. The list of frustrations for Adir and his efforts to rebuild were mounting. Every time he attempted to reconstruct the life he and Elgo once had, it was if they struggled all the more. At bedtime, sleep would be stymied by relentless judgments about what was not working. The first thing Adir thought about in the morning would be the rebuilding obstacles in front of them. Where would they get the finances to rebuild? Where would the materials come from? Who would take their support elsewhere with other creatures carrying on with their lives while Adir and Elgo continued to flounder?

Despite Adir's attempts to dig deep and summon his signature willpower, it wasn't working. Or, more accurately, it would work for a while, but felt limited. In the morning, he would push aside doubts, but he seemed to meet one roadblock after another throughout the day. Clients wouldn't answer his messages. His willpower was like a battery that can only last for a period of time.

Adir would look back at his Notes to Self when he and Elgo had been trying to reach the Oasis those many years ago. Inscribed in his notebook, he read, "Let me get this straight. Willpower is a conscious decision to keep going by the power of thought. Elephants are driven by emotion. Elgo is no exception. He responds to my will to keep going. But, despite my best efforts, his frustration keeps bubbling to the surface. Elgo has these pesky patterns of limiting beliefs. In other words, he lacks confidence. Could it be he thinks he doesn't deserve to reach the Oasis? What is it with my elephant that he seems to stand in the way of my willpower and positivity? I must ask Brio about this."

Adir looked at his entry and wondered if history was repeating itself after the earthquake—as they faced the aftereffects from the earthquake. Was Elgo allowing old patterns of doubt and fear of uncertainty to control his emotions again? Adir wondered if the willpower that was famous for lifting twenty times his body weight was pointless when pitted against the deep recesses of self-doubt in the darker side of his elephant's habitual ways.

Adir grumbled to himself, "Define the problem. Aim my efforts. Succeed with relentless force." It worked in the past. He resolved to make it work again. He sat up on Elgo's back. He—and Elgo—would align and get moving.

"What do you think, Elgo? Shall we shake this off? Shall we stay in the Oasis and rebuild our lives?"

Adir and Elgo's inseparable connection was an interesting dynamic. Elgo needed Adir to interpret the world around them. Adir needed Elgo to align with his ant's leadership of the self. They were both driven by habits. But changing bad habits was easier for Adir than Elgo. If Adir realized that picking up twigs with his middle two legs was easier than using his front two, he would adapt readily. But, as history proved again and again, Elgo's habits were sometimes formed over a lifetime. Elgo had grown up in a pretty negative environment. His uncles, Nega and Holic, were poster elephants for "What could go wrong, will go wrong." It took the guidance of Adir and the mentorship of Brio to slowly bury the old habits of dread and doubt. Adir sensed that Elgo was slipping insidiously back into his dysfunctional ways. Elgo was truly a creature of habit. He was not wired to interpret information. His behavior was 100 percent formed by his past experiences. Elgo's patterns of behavior, his habits, were a well-worn path that he would naturally fall into. If negativity was that well-worn way, then that was his way. Adir felt what smacked of an anti–elephant buzz. A sense of slipping into a listless, numb feeling pervaded.

Adir straightened his back further, while fighting his growing agitation for misalignment with his elephant. Again, he doubled down on his self-talk.

"Define the problem. Aim my efforts." He couldn't feel Elgo responding. In fact, he felt no feelings back from his elephant. Adir blurted out, "Nothing. Nothing! NOTHING?"

Adir started to shake. Standing in place was untenable. A walk would do them good.

"C'mon, Elgo. Let's walk."

Five steps into their walk, Elgo slipped on loose, wet rock. Due to the contour changes caused by the earthquake, what was once a rolling hill had fractured into a steep drop-off. They began careening down the slope. Adir's tiny body catapulted off Elgo as they both tumbled into a chaotic acceleration downhill.

Of all the places to slip, this was about the worst. The farther they fell, the faster they went.

Adir reached out one of his legs to control his fall. Instead, it hyperextended, leaving a searing pain shooting through his thorax.

He tried reaching out with a different leg. The results were nearly identical—a shooting pain through his midsection—except this leg hurt worse. Bad enough that Adir wondered if he'd broken it. But he still needed to stop his fall. He tried to grab with his other four legs. Branches skewered his body and shredded his appendages to raw tissue. Nothing he did stopped his fall. While Elgo tumbled alongside him, Adir was only aware of his own grunting and groaning.

Finally, at the bottom of the ruptured embankment, they thump-thumped to a stop. Adir felt like a compressed pile of twisted and banged-up ant. He looked around and noticed how Elgo was already sitting upright. His buddy seemed unscathed. Strange. A twenty-thousand-pound elephant should have hit even more obstacles on their free fall, but only Adir seemed impacted.*

Adir, in pain, did a self-scan, patting all body parts with all six feet. Nothing was broken. No feet were pointed in the wrong direction. No ant blood. Just stem to stern, total body soreness. He turned to look at his elephant. "Let's make our way back to the trail, Elgo." Adir didn't have time for this painful interruption. He had pressing rebuilding problems he had to deal with. He tried to hobble back over to Elgo. Both his middle leg on his left side and his front leg on his right side were torridly painful. They'd hyperextended and were next to useless. The more throbbing he felt, the more frustrated he became. "I don't have time for this,"

---

* Gravity's a bugger sometimes.

he grunted. Elgo didn't know whether to move closer to Adir or wait until his ant's next move.

Adir's body kept betraying him. His front right ankle could take only partial weight, so he sat back down to fashion a twig into a cross between a splint and a prosthetic, thinking it would support his weight as he edged himself closer to Elgo. Adir then grabbed a suitable walking stick, assuming it would support his weight. With one hop-step, the twig broke and he slammed down on the right side of his face. A knot formed on his temple.

"Arrgggghhhhh! What is going on?!?"

"When disaster strikes, be open to a solution," murmured a voice—one that Adir knew.

When disaster **strikes,**
be **open** to a **solution.**

He snapped his head around, wrenching it out of the dirt.

Adir purged his thoughts without taking a breath. He spoke in a continuous stream of frustration. "Brio?! Brio! Did you see what happened? I'm a mess. I can't seem to get my thoughts straight. Not only do I feel like I'm flailing in the dark, I just fell three hundred feet, all while bouncing and being whacked around like I was in a pinball machine. What is going on? Why am I a basket case? It feels like no matter what I do, I'm doing the opposite . . . no, that sounds absurd. I'm doing everything I need to do. I know I am! But everything hurts. My legs. My body. My life . . ." Adir's voice trailed off as he drew air back into his lungs. His next few breaths diminished into a desperate sigh.

"My dear friend, you just fell into a lesson you need to learn. I'm here to help."

There was a long silence as Adir tried to think past the pain to what Brio was referring to.

"Nice to see you, Brio. How's life? How are the kids? How's the arthritis? Did you know there was a FREAKING EARTH-QUAKE and everything has gone to hell?" Adir couldn't dial back his intensity.

"Indeed. It has been quite a setback for everyone. But let's get back to you." Brio's calm only minutely helped Adir feel less stressed.

As Adir limped onto Elgo's back, Brio perched in front of the elephant. With a sturdier walking stick Adir had found on the ground, the ant started pacing in hobbled, erratic pivots. Adir stopped mid-grumble, took a sideways glance at Brio, inhaled slowly, and then slumped into a pile of frustration, ready to listen.

With a confident, deliberate tenor, the owl mentor spoke directly to the ant. "Adir, my cherished ant friend, when disaster struck, you instinctively tried to impose a solution. Those instincts might have been a natural part of who you are, or you might have developed them over time as part of your character traits, but I'm willing to bet that you've been operating on your character instincts since the earthquake shook the Oasis." Brio must have seen the question in Adir's eyes, because he continued even before the ant could ask. "Your injuries tell me that you're not operating under natural instincts. You see, it's some character instincts that can end up blocking a solution. Natural instincts can save your life or point you in the right direction, but character instincts can be a tad more stubborn. If you or I get injured, our strength of character has us push through the pain. When we are in a hole, we stubbornly force our way to get back on top. And when we fall, we fight it all the way.

"As you fell down the side of this slope, you were fighting a losing battle against gravity. By resisting, you hurt your arms and ankle. Your elephant didn't resist the fall and came out unharmed. It's no different in life.

"Do not let some of those troublesome, stubborn character instincts get in the way of a solution to a devastating incident. When devastation gets in the way, through the middle of it is the way.

> When **devastation** gets *in the way*,
> through the **middle of it** is the way.

"Instead of stubbornly resisting challenge, ease into the space of that very challenge. That which you resist will persist. Hear this, Adir: If you're injured, rest. If you're in a hole, pace yourself. If gravity or a force outside of you, like the aftershocks from an earthquake, has taken over and you're falling, go with it. Don't panic; embrace the unknown. Have faith over force.

If you're **injured**, rest.
If you're **in a hole**, pace yourself.
If you're **falling**, go with it.

"Adir, all this pushing, forcing, and resisting is putting you deeper in a hole—both physically and mentally. You're making things worse for yourself. Stop doing that starting now. Rest for a bit. Pace yourself. Go with the flow."

Elgo smiled. He heard a universal truth, which had him grinning from ear to floppy ear. Adir, though, just nodded and relaxed his jaw. For a quick moment, the fight in Adir's nature gave way to Brio's sage advice, and the ant let go.

Elgo rose from the crouch he'd adopted when letting Adir climb onto his back. He took both Adir and Brio up the hill. No words were spoken as their thoughts occupied their mental space.

The next morning, Adir shook off the fall, resolving himself to avoid compounding the devastation of the earthquake with worries about a little setback like falling down the hill. He arose, knowing he had work to do—that he had to adjust himself to a new reality and figure out his new solution. He took a stack of birch sheets as a brand-new notebook and a charred sliver of wood as his pencil. If he were to stop feeling like everything was a struggle, he would need a technique he had used to get to the Oasis in the first place. This notebook would help him find a way to thrive in the post-earthquake Oasis. He paused to think, then wrote down ideas Brio had said surrounding setbacks and breakthroughs.

ADIR'S NOTES TO SELF

- When devastation gets in the way, through the middle of it is the way.
- When disaster strikes, be open to a solution.
- If I'm falling, go with it. If I'm injured, rest. If I'm in a hole, pace myself.

CHAPTER 2

Using Discomfort as a Catalyst

With the morning light still breaking the muted tones of a dark sky, Adir finished writing in his notebook and realized how stiff he was from the fall the day before. Because he had to move slower, he took notice of a sign he normally scuttled right by. He had bought it at the local market a few years ago because it featured a quote that reminded him of how he and his large friend, Elgo, found the Oasis in the first place. It said:

The **path** of self-discovery
is **before you**.

Now, though, his aversion to heading out on any path at all made his stubborn gene take over. *"The Oasis is where I am meant to be. I have succeeded in the past. I didn't make this lifestyle we had by using Brio's 'Go with the flow' advice. I willed my elephant to this place. I have won in the past and I will win in the future. It is how I roll."*

The weeks passed as they rebuilt their home on a patch of more solid ground on the same high vantage overlooking the Oasis. He had Elgo fashion a water catchment for when it rained. Adir was determined to re-create his forever home in the location of his dreams. In addition, he relentlessly fought to put more numbers in the profit side of his business ledger rather than the mounting debt in the loss column. He could feel pressure from others to make a change. Should he pivot off his consulting practice and onto a new business? What would that business be? Should he find a new job? Should he give up on rebuilding his dream property and leave the Oasis? He didn't want to leave the location of his dreams, despite the fact that it no longer resembled the paradise that he'd long imagined.

Adir didn't even realize that he was ignoring Brio's advice, even as other animals flowed away from their Oasis homes. He didn't see that he'd closed himself off to other solutions as summer faded into fall.

The change in the valley from green to vibrant orange and red lit up Adir's view from the windows of his makeshift home.

It was difficult to recognize the devastation from just a few months back.

Adir asked Elgo to bend down and have a closer look at a perfect autumn-colored leaf. As they bent, a blast of heavy breathing and a flurry of predatory paws nearby sent Adir and Elgo into hiding, pinning themselves up against an outcropping of rock to remain out of sight.

"This can't be," Adir murmured to Elgo. As winter closed the door to fall, wolves would migrate toward their prey at lower altitudes, but it was still fall. Adir's mind raced. He'd known he would have to protect himself and his colony in a few weeks, but these wolves were early.

As screams of fear and desperation reached his ears, Adir realized he and Elgo weren't the only ones caught off guard. What was happening to their neighbors?

Then, as quickly as they had come, the wolves were gone. It had been a quick mission to scout out what remained in the Oasis.

The rest of the day saw what was left of the colony in the Oasis devolve into despair and choruses of, "What do we do? Where do we go? Everyone who left for the port must be thriving. We have nothing to keep us here. We must leave or perish."

The next morning, the entire community was on alert. Most animals wanted to flee, having given up the stubbornness that'd made them cling to the Oasis even as others left in the aftermath of the earthquake. But now they couldn't. Fear of another attack paralyzed them, as they worried that the wolves would return while they were defenseless and leaving the Oasis.

The wolves did return. They sniffed out their victims. More screams. More panic.

The pack had surrounded its prey, a young deer separated from her herd. The kill was out of sight from Adir and Elgo's standpoint, but no less scarring. They froze in place and did not dare to move.

From Adir and Elgo's vantage point above, the pack of wolves whooshed past. The lead wolf had a limp doe in his fangs. As it dragged the lifeless body up the trail, the pack followed. The morbid chaos subsided. Adir turned to his catatonic colony and insisted everyone stay put while he and Elgo checked out the surroundings. With Adir on Elgo's back, they wound down the switchbacks that led to the main Oasis trail. As they rounded the final corner, they stopped dead. The pack of wolves could still be seen making their way back to their mountain wilderness.

One lone wolf, a sweeper designated to guard the back of the pack during retreats, turned its head and caught sight of Adir and Elgo.

This was the end, and they knew it.

The wolf had one blue eye and one brown eye, but both were fierce with menace.

It glanced up the trail at the rest of the pack as they rounded the next bend. The air was unnaturally quiet. The wolf paused, considering whether to follow the pack, which was eager to feed.

It turned back to Adir and Elgo, who were still motionless. It came back within earshot. The wolf lowered its head and growled a message they would never forget.

"I . . . will . . . return. The blood of your young friend is still warm, and I'm hungry. But I will return."

The wolf, enjoying the torment it was causing the ant and the elephant, took a few steps toward them.

"My name is Chromia," it uttered with a growl. "You can't hide. If you do, I'll sniff you out. Then," it said while baring its fangs, "my pack will feast on your flesh. You have the night to say your goodbyes."

"Mr. Chromia—"

"Ms.!" she barked. "*Ms.* Chromia!"

"M-M-Ms. Chromia, would you maybe consider not coming back?"

The wolf's blue eye glinted. "What's your name?"

Adir gulped.

"*What's your name?*" she growled.

"My name is Adir. This is Elgo—he doesn't talk. We're pleased to meet y . . ." Adir's voice trailed off.

Chromia looked back up the trail, paused in thought, then turned her gaze directly back into Elgo's eyes. "Boys, I have mouths to feed and this mute elephant will be our next dinner. And you, little ant, I'll kill you just for the sport of it. Remember this, I always get what I want. No matter what gets in my way. Once I decide on something, I'll never let it go. You can't escape me." She stepped back, raised one lip, and exposed a bloody fang. "I eat *struggle* for breakfast."

As she turned to catch up to the pack, she left one last parting shot: "I will not let go."

With an upturned tail and thick, stiff fur accentuating her powerful shoulders, she bounded up the trail to join her pack. In a half-second, she was gone.

Adir and Elgo let out the breaths it felt like they'd held for the entire exchange.

Let's go! They ran back up to their friends and colony who had undoubtedly heard every bit of Chromia's threat.

They had been hanging on in the Oasis, stubbornly expecting things to get back to normal. There would be no return to normal. Normal no longer existed. They had to gather up whatever their colony could carry and leave.

In the flurry of activity of "keep or leave behind," Adir slowed down long enough to pick up the small sign about the path and self-discovery. He set it back down with the message facing up. He looked at the eastern path out of the Oasis. He imagined that the path to self-discovery was waiting for them.

"Elgo, this sign says, 'The path of self-discovery is before you.' We may not know what awaits us on this path." He then waved across the expanse of the broken Oasis. "I've been thinking," he said while patting the back of Elgo's broad brow with his front free hand. He looked back at the Oasis and pondered how instantly irrelevant it was. "Buddy, you never know what's next until you encounter what isn't. And this Oasis," he said, waving his right two arms across the dry valley below, "isn't!"

Adir felt Elgo shudder in fear and uncertainty.

Adir interpreted the elephant's feelings. "Elgo, I don't know what's next. But this place is no longer our Oasis. Even if we glue together our shattered dreams, they will still never be the same. I've been too stubborn. We must let go and leave this broken place behind. We are forced to create a new reality, a new solution."

You never **know** what's **next**
until you **encounter** what isn't.
Re-create a new reality.

The rest of the colony was in agreement. They had survived two encounters with the wolves, but it was time to move on before Chromia and her pack returned and finished them and Elgo off.

Packing up their things and putting young ones on their shoulders, they headed off in the exact opposite direction from the Western Mountains. Adir settled in on Elgo's back and reached for his birch notepad. He scanned the previous entries and wondered what he needed to learn next. As he jotted down his reminders, to no one but himself, he hoped they would contribute to his self-discovery. He looked over at his community and felt what they were feeling. They didn't know exactly where they were going to end up; they only knew their direction started on the eastbound trail.

ADIR'S NOTES TO SELF

- The path of self-discovery is before me.
- The more stubborn I am, the more I will struggle with letting go.
- I'll never know what's next until I encounter what *isn't*.
- Discomfort will force me to create a new reality.

CHAPTER 3

Harnessing Action to Interrupt Anxiety

For the first few miles of their journey, Adir, Elgo, and their friends followed a well-traveled trail but, knowing that Chromia and her pack would sniff out their location, when they came across Mill Creek, they tromped through the water to erase their scent.

As they trekked, crisp air gave way to intermittent sunshine, though clouds and wind swirled in a precursor to less friendly weather. By the time the refugees found a flat area between a small overhang, the creek, and a forest of green cactus, a snow squall had descended on them. It was strange because snow was not expected for a couple of months. This was just Mother Nature reminding everyone who was in charge.

The displaced party pulled the lower vines away from the outcropping to fashion a colorful curtain against the storm. The cliff overhead combined with the screen of vines allowed a substantial dry area that undulated with four "rooms" of sorts. The middle area would be ideal for a common area and a fire to stay warm. The side areas would work for sleeping quarters. The farthest space had a narrow cascade of water that meandered into the patch of outgrowth. Higher ground on either side of the creek was festooned with deep green cacti and shrubs dusted with the early snowfall.

Their abode was secure yet well lit because of its north-facing opening.

The scurry of settling in and situating their own personal space eventually dissipated into a quiet murmur. Some sat in a circle and recounted the adventure they had just experienced. Others hung their heads, remembering the young deer snatched by the marauding wolves. Elgo sat on his haunches and rested his back on the dry cliff wall. Despite the vast space, everyone huddled together in closer proximity than necessary. They found comfort in closeness while staying relatively warm compared to the brisk air outside the enclosure.

For everyone, it felt good to stop moving after a day that had begun with their lives in peril, continued with a burst of packing, and ended with an escape. Only now could each member of the group slip into an exhausted sleep.

Adir's mind was still darting from one anxious thought to the next. He heard his companions descend into sleep, their breathing evening out one by one as they found the kind of peace that only comes when consciousness needs a break. Adir knew it was a kind of peace they had not felt in the months since the wreckage from the earthquake.

For Adir, thoughts of uncertainty were soon replaced with thoughts of failure. He could feel Elgo stir amid a fitful sleep.

Why was I not able to figure out how to turn things around?

The more he settled into the quiet, the less settled he felt. He began to shake, as if panicked, but that didn't seem right since there was nothing he could see to panic about.

He started talking to himself.

Adir, stop feeling as if you're the victim. That's a place of powerlessness.

But the earthquake was not my fault.

The economy of the Oasis's business standstill, not my fault.

The wolves prowling early, not my fault.

What am I missing? What can I do to turn this around?

But it's not my fault was his last thought before he, too, took a deep breath and slipped into a state between wakefulness and sleep. His mind cascaded from one involuntary imagined experience to the next. He was chased by creatures in the shadows.

He was unable to move high up in a tree. He was lost in a vast expanse. He was stuck, unable to move forward or back. He was flying, then falling from the sky.

Stop being the victim.
This is a place of powerlessness.

As morning unfolded, everyone reoriented to their new haven. They decided to call it "the Vine Spot." It became increasingly obvious that this location had merit. Their spot was neither traceable nor apparent to a pack of hungry, cheesed-off wolves. Over the course of a few days, the colony settled in. They pulled more vines down. Some of the vines were perennials. These star jasmines and climbing hydrangeas added to the autumn aroma of their new enclosure. Moreover, any trace of their scent would further confound wolves scouring for their location. In all, their spot helped them feel safe.

The Vine Spot had water, a barricade of spiked sentries, a dry, warm, shielded platform, plus plenty of space to forage for food. Their only locational weakness was from the air, and winged predators were the only animal they now feared.

But, with fall opening for winter, the hazards associated with birds of prey were nonexistent, so they settled in for daily routines of homeschooling, seeking food stores, and living hand-to-mouth. The colony saw Adir lead their survival tasks. But inside,

Adir was struggling, becoming increasingly uncomfortable the more the colony invested in their spot. At times, he didn't even want to get out of bed. Anxiety came in waves, but he told no one. This was not a time for weakness. He needed to be strong.

Despite the early snowfall on their first day in their new location, fall and then winter were unseasonably warm. Little to no snow fell over the course of time. The days were mild and accommodating, cold coming only briefly at night. By late winter, Adir and Elgo had slipped into a routine, but there were unsettling discrepancies manifesting in their reactions to their new surroundings.

Elgo was comfortable in his habitual yet sometimes mysterious ways, but Adir was normally a driven, compulsive, and focused individual. It became his turn to have surges of anxiety. Adir would obsess about his setbacks and failures. Every day he would have to shake off the insidious thought that he might have lost his "conquer any obstacle" mojo.

He abided this new home, but couldn't shake the sense that he had let his colony down. He couldn't believe what he'd been reduced to despite his past successes. Was he incapable of ever bouncing back?

Elgo listened whenever Adir complained. He heard all of Adir's caustic mutterings, locking each of them into his memory. The thousands of times that Adir repeated himself buried the negative message into Elgo.

Adir didn't even realize that he was constantly implanting negativity in Elgo's memory banks. Meanwhile, Adir never fully realized that he was not in control.

When they'd made their home in the Oasis, they'd been able to do it because of Adir's constant positive self-talk. Yet now, Adir didn't even register how far he'd slipped on the slope of negativity. Instead of being the steward of deliberate positivity, Adir was feeding Elgo a toxic diet of self-doubt, frustration, and hopelessness.

Communication between any ant and elephant is a one-way street. When the ant isn't the architect of a positive and clearly aligned dominant thought, then any progress is folly. Adir couldn't see the form of self-destruction his stubborn fixation on having all the answers was having on his elephantine subconscious. Until he let go of this fixation, this bias would be a constant source of frustration and stuckness.

Adir obsessed over his discontent. He thought to himself, "I feel like I'm tolerating this 'living hand-to-mouth.' Sure, we're surviving, but I want us to thrive. This could go on for years. Decades! Ugh. Why can't I figure out how to get out of this 'sell-out to just exist'? Why won't Elgo give off a more positive vibe? Does he not want bigger and better things? Why won't he just listen to me and change?"

Adir, like the average individual, experienced around 65,000 thoughts per day. With thousands of them focused on bemoaning Adir's losses, Elgo couldn't help but be impacted. The more frustrated Adir became, the more Elgo was programmed to make dysfunction the new normal. The chasm between Adir's drive and Elgo's expectation for "settling for less" grew until, eventually, Adir's ambition and Elgo's limiting beliefs placed a chasm between them.

Adir looked across the colony on a day that seemed like the day before and the day before that. He pulled out his notebook and wrote:

> Repeated **frustration** ends
> up being the new **normal**.

He punched his makeshift scribing utensil as the period after "normal." The nub snapped off and he stared at his broken pencil. As he fished around for another carbon tip, his mind wandered to the horizon across the field of cactus.

This process of simply trying to eke out an existence was corroding any feelings of joy. Adir grew tormented by their new reality, and this subsistence conflicted Elgo. He clearly liked the security but felt misaligned with his ant. The more Adir pushed for progress, the less connected Elgo felt with Adir. Adir wanted to explore while Elgo resisted any thoughts of adventure. They were stuck.

Adir opened his notebook to a new page. He didn't want dysfunction to become his "new normal." He wanted to ensure he put into action the notes he took, the lessons he was learning.

Maybe by writing down his ideas, he would find a way to get through to Elgo. At a deep level, he felt his Notes to Self would gain some traction in his everyday life. He trusted these notes would help him get past any feelings of panic that seemed to be germinating in his head and heart.

ADIR'S NOTES TO SELF

- Stop feeling like a victim. That's a place of powerlessness.
- Say something a thousand times, and it is locked in a thousand times.
- The more frustrated I become, the more I am programmed to make dysfunction the new normal.
- Keep looking for what I need to let go of.

CHAPTER 4

Letting Go of the Right Way

A dir closed his notebook and looked up at the hanging vines. He was startled enough to drop his pencil and pad when he heard Brio's voice: "If you're trying to hide, you should know that the two massive elephant feet sticking out of a wall of vines give you away." Elgo pulled his legs into a cross-legged position.

"Huh. Ya. Good point," replied Adir as he adjusted to hearing a voice that wasn't his own. "It's good to see you, Brio. Pull up a patch of elephant hide. Let's talk."

Brio complied while Adir continued on. "Listen, I've got a bunch of thoughts rattling around in my brain. How much time do you have?"

"I'm yours for the day. What's up?"

"Do you remember how, when Elgo and I were first trying to get to the Oasis, I used Gold Dots as a reminder of our goal?" asked Adir.

"Gold Dots?" asked Brio.

"You know, remember how I used pollen spores as reminders for Elgo's and my goal to get to the Oasis? I called those Gold Dots and used them as triggers to remind us of something that was bigger than just a goal. These Gold Dots represented the elephant buzz that excited us. We would see a golden spore and we trained ourselves to go through the five senses of what we imagined in the Oasis. The sounds of the wind brushing through the trees and a waterfall in the distance. The colors of the trees and the blue pond below. Although this was all in our minds, we could feel the textures of the ground beneath our feet and the sweet taste of orange, ripe mangoes that hung all around us. When we rounded off the five senses with the smells of pine trees and honeysuckle, we would get that delicious feeling of alignment. In our very being we experienced a setting that just hadn't happened yet. A simple Gold Dot would trigger real-as-life feelings of gratitude, satisfaction, and joy. Each Gold Dot sighting would cause Elgo to shudder. That's why we called it an elephant buzz. The Gold Dot was a reminder, much like 'north' is on a compass. We knew exactly what we needed to find. We used it as a tool to follow your advice."

"What advice was that?" Brio said with an encouraging tone.

"You will gravitate toward your current dominant thought. Be the architect of that dominant thought. Our Gold Dots keep us aligned with each other."

Brio's voice interrupted Adir's musings. "Well done, you two. I'll be sure to remember the Gold Dot technique for triggering a dominant thought. They are the perfect reminders of the value of staying on track."

"But now it's different with the Gold Dots." Adir's voice sounded as distraught as he felt. "Since we've been camped at this Vine Spot, I resurrected the Gold Dot technique because our dominant thoughts are far from healthy or leading to any form of progress. In fact, I felt like we were 180 degrees of misalignment. I figured Gold Dots would snap us out of a feeling of powerlessness. I thought about our next Oasis. I imagined a place that would be my ultimate dream home. What could be better than a place overlooking a pond in the Oasis? 'How about a Mansion by the Ocean?' I thought to myself. I decided to make this my dominant thought."

"It sounds like you are driving toward a thing rather than a way of life," said Brio. "Accumulating things is not nearly as good a motivator as a life well lived."

"But I'm not! It's much more than a thing. I bring in the five senses to a setting that checks all sorts of 'life-well-lived' boxes. The sounds of the surf and kids playing near the waves. The feeling and sights of standing on the balcony with my future wife.

I can feel her—she has her front right *hand* on the left side of my thorax. Her warmth couples with the warm sunshine baking our right side. I can see a reflection in the glass of balcony doors, showing our healthy, toned bodies as we toast with champagne to our debt-free abode. The smells of the ocean meet the aroma of the vibrant green trees all around us. There is a creek to our right. I can hear it between waves caressing the shores. The feelings of gratitude, satisfaction, and joy are all part of this experience of our Mansion by the Ocean."

"That's a heck of a Gold Dot. What's Elgo's reaction when you experience it in your imagination?" Brio seemed on board with the imagery.

"Well, this is where it gets weird. In the beginning of our time at the Vine Spot, Elgo definitely liked the future reality of everyone together at the Mansion on the Ocean. But, over time, he stopped giving off an elephant buzz. Now, I see the Gold Dots, and nothing happens. I activate all five senses and conjure up gratitude, satisfaction, and joy. But I'm just met with a dud. Nothing."

"What's happening with Elgo's thoughts, Adir?"

"You tell me. I have no idea."

Brio tilted his head and pondered. "To be honest, I'd say if a Gold Dot is not resonating with your elephant, you don't have the right Gold Dot trigger. Doesn't it make more sense to get your elephant's mindset cleaned up and stable before you can effectively set out on a new direction? If you force your decisions on your elephant, you'll both just end up frustrated. You may fixate on the solutions being related to one destination while Elgo may be satisfied with a different station in life. The more you fixate on 'your way,' the further you will find yourself from proper alignment in your relationship with Elgo.

"Until you embrace the opposition between your 'right way' and your partner's 'right way,' you'll never be able to sync with Elgo for a solution."

Two "right ways" will never sync up. Collaborate for a solution.

"W-w-w-wait up there, Mr. B." Adir held up a finger.* "First of all, I actually know my way is the right way." He raised a second finger. "Second of all, Elgo and I can collaborate when he accepts that I know what's good for both of us."

Brio blinked. He rotated his head nearly 180 degrees behind him, then returned his gaze to Adir. "Let's have a little lesson, shall we?"

Adir nodded. Brio's lessons always changed his life in positive ways. He leaned forward, knowing he was about to get exactly what he needed.

"You see the field of cactus out over my shoulders?" Brio waited for Adir to nod before continuing. "How long do you think they've been there? Years?"

---

* Ants have multiple fingers. Who knew?

"I'd say decades," replied Adir.

"And these vines?"

"Shoot, I bet these crawlers grew fairly recently. You can tell by the width of their stalks."

"A cactus is stationary and prickly. Its roots are shallow, and it has no intention of going anywhere. Its prickly exterior keeps it safe and alive. It has a fixed mindset. A vine, on the other hand, is curious. It has a growth mindset. It seeks the light. It looks for new pathways and never seems to stop growing. It's like it embraces uncertainty rather than suffer in safety. It thrives from growth."

"Who said I'm suffering?" Adir didn't want to admit it, but he was. Wasn't anxiety a form of suffering?

"Are you happy? Is Elgo happy? Is everyone happy, or are they more stuck in place, safe but quietly suffering? Silent suffering can become a habit. Some habits are absolutely not worth keeping."

Silent **suffering** can become a **habit**.
Some habits are absolutely
not worth keeping.

Adir could feel the truth in Brio's words. Elgo was clearly listening, too. "I think this suffering has become an unfortunate habit," admitted Adir. "I hate to say it, but it smacks of an addiction to suffering. Is that possible?"

"Not only is addiction to negative thinking possible, it can be part of every ant and elephant's everyday existence. The worst part is, you don't know it's an addiction until someone from the outside points it out. You don't notice what you don't notice. Adir. Elgo. You have an addiction to suffering, and it's your choice to stop this pattern of thinking."

"How?" asked Adir while Elgo leaned forward.

"It's time to get comfortable with being uncomfortable."

"Actually . . ." Adir cleared his throat. "I *am* uncomfortable. We suffer and it seems normal. I try to formulate a new Gold Dot for a new elephant buzz, and there's no alignment with Elgo. I can't seem to find a new path or a new Gold Dot for us that is worth chasing. I struggle, and thoughts of that struggle consume me. I start suffering in this negativity, and Elgo doesn't like it, either. But the feeling spirals down, farther and farther."

"To stop this downward spiral, I suggest you interrupt the pattern and change your focus."

"How?" repeated Adir.

"Let's try this," said Brio, couching his next words carefully. "Would you say you love to be right?"

"Yes. But everyone loves to be right," said Adir, defending himself reflexively.

"True," replied Brio. "Everyone loves to be right. In fact, it is a fixation on being right. It can be a blind-spot bias that people don't even realize they have."

A fixation on being right can be a blind-spot bias people don't even realize they have.

"What's a blind-spot bias?" asked Adir.

"May I borrow your notebook and pencil for a moment?" asked Brio.

Adir handed the items to Brio, who scribbled two dots on a blank page.

●   ●

"Now cover your right eye," Brio instructed. "Focus your attention at the right dot. Slowly bring the notepad closer to your face. At some point, the left dot will disappear."

Adir did as he was told, then blurted out, "Wait a minute. It disappeared. I didn't know I had a blind spot."

"Most creatures don't know they have a blind spot until it's pointed out. Most creatures don't know they have a blind-spot bias until the bias is pointed out. It stands to reason 'being right' might be a bias you don't even know you have."

Brio stood his ground and continued, "Please take a moment to actually think about what I'm about to ask you: Are you assuming the same character traits that got you to your dream of living in the Oasis will get you to your new Mansion by the Ocean?"

Adir considered the somewhat pointless question. "If you're asking about my resolve, then I am not *assuming* I know how to get past this existence where I'm barely scraping by. I *know* I know how to get out of this mess because, for years, I've known how to achieve absolutely any and every goal."

"So . . ." Brio stared at Adir with unblinking eyes. "You know you're right because you've done it before. You have a bias that you know what needs to be done."

"Right," said Adir, slowly realizing he was talking about a possible blind-spot bias he didn't know he had.

"What if what got you to the Oasis will not work on this next journey? What if your 5Cs of Clarity of Vision, Commitment, Consistency, Confidence, and Control don't work when there is a massive setback, like an earth-shattering earthquake?" Brio leaned forward to continue. "You've experienced an unimaginable amount of chaos, and there is no linear way out of chaos. There's no direct path. No straightforward formula that will march you out of that chaos."

Adir had an epiphany. He realized his bias for what he "knew" to be true was not working. He didn't know how to get unstuck. He didn't know the solution. His very bias for achieving any goal he set his mind to was what was indeed keeping him stuck in chaos.

Brio interrupted Adir's thoughts with another question. "Do you know how you are directly adding to the chaos?"

"*I'm* adding to my chaos? I just realized by holding on to my bias, I'm holding myself back. Now you're saying I'm making it worse?"

Brio blinked and kept staring at his friends.

"How am I adding to this chaos? Where? In what way?" Adir was desperate for answers.

"What self-talk are you giving Elgo?"

"'We can do this. Don't give up. Go this way,'" Adir responded.

"Are you saying there's no confusion in your self-talk? Nothing like, 'Why is this happening to me?' or 'What am I missing?' or 'I've lost my ability to succeed'?" Brio let these words hang in the air.

Adir realized that's exactly what he was doing: communicating confusion, uncertainty, and limiting beliefs to Elgo through his growing frustration.

Elgo raised an eyebrow and rested his jaw on his bent front leg to stare at Adir.

Adir looked at Elgo, back to Brio, back to Elgo, then down. They'd hit a nerve. A wave of sadness washed over Adir.

The impact of his self-talk came crashing down, as did the realization that his corrosive inner dialogue—"How could this happen?"—was influencing Elgo. Maybe that's why Elgo wasn't responding to the Mansion by the Ocean Gold Dot . . .

"Let go of your blind-spot bias. Embrace the possibility of a path that neither of you can see now. It's time to embrace uncertainty. Allow humility to chart your alignment with your partner."

Allow **humility** to chart your *path*
of **alignment** with your **partner**.

"Embrace uncertainty like these vines do as they keep exploring?"

"Yes." Brio carefully gathered his next words. "This earth-quake you experienced has created pure chaos. Those many years ago, when you and Elgo found your way to your Oasis, you engaged in a step-by-step process. First, you *clarified your vision* of living in the Oasis. Then you *committed* to the search for that dream location across the Savannah. Next, you *consistently* moved west from your humble beginnings. You built *confidence* along the way and *controlled* how you stayed on track."

"Right," said Adir. "Back then, there was no chaos. There were obstacles and challenges along the way but it was a linear, step-by-step sequence of clarity, commitment, consistency, confidence, and control. These five Cs just aren't working. We have no clarity. No commitment. No consistency. No confidence, and especially, NO CONTROL. We are living in chaos, and my assumptions, or biases, as you say, are not working."

"Awareness sets the stage for learning, Adir. You are aware that your elephant has no equilibrium. He is off balance. Your elephant is getting mixed messages. Even worse, the more nega-tive thoughts you inject into him, the more he will be inclined to hold on to anything secure such as this hand-to-mouth existence, even if it is going nowhere. Your elephantine subconscious friend has changed. Only peace of mind, an awareness that you don't have the answers—and the humility to accept that and let go—will put you on the path to better methods of aligning Elgo with what is truly going to escape this frustration."

Brio paused long enough to worry Adir. "I hate to say it, but there's worse news about why you're feeling stuck."

Adir thought to himself that everything comes in threes. "What's this next bit of bad news?" he mused. After a few seconds of reflection, he said to Brio, "Stuck is an understatement." He looked around to make sure no one could hear. His tone hushed, he confided, "I feel panicked. Right after we arrived at the Vine Spot, I sat in a corner and just started shaking. All I could do was hide, shake, and feel powerless.

"I *never* feel panic. But here I am confused, stuck, and super anxious. I have to force myself to get up and move."

"That's to be expected. You've gone through the three classic stages everyone experiences after an earthquake in their lives. First, you lived through the chaos of the earthquake. Second, you valiantly fought the massive setback in your life. You looked for ways to fight the aftershocks. Now you're on the third, caught in post-trauma stress. You are literally in a form of shock."

"Shock?" echoed Adir, trying to understand.

"Think of it this way: Along your travels, a pack of hyenas attacks your colony. First, you experience the chaos of the attack. Then, you fight. Finally, after you've escaped disaster, the adrenaline wears off. You seize up from shock. You get the shakes. You find you can't do anything but stare straight ahead in disbelief . . ."

"That's exactly what I've been thinking all along—how can this happen to me? I couldn't wrap my mind around how I had what it takes to conquer all the obstacles along the way to our haven in the Oasis. I had what it took to build a successful life for us in our dream location. But then this earthquake changed everything, and I felt like I devolved rather than evolved."

"No matter how strong someone is, they'll experience three stages as part of a devastating event. Stage 1: Your Personal Earthquake. Stage 2: You Fight. Stage 3: Your Post-traumatic Anxiety."

Adir thought over his own experiences after the earthquake. For all these months, he'd been *fighting*. Fighting to rebuild. Fighting the setbacks and the fall. Fighting to survive long enough to escape Chromia and her wolf pack. After finally being able to rest at the Vine Spot, the feelings of uncontrollable anxiety, self-doubt, and debilitating panic began.

Brio spoke gently, softly, afraid to spook Adir. "It doesn't matter how strong and determined an ant is—we all have times where a traumatic setback takes over. Allow this moment of fragility to pass. Fragile items need to be handled with care. Take the time and the self-compassion to care for yourself, Adir."

Adir's eyes began to water. For the first time in his life, he decided to give himself a break. He hung his head. But this time, not in despair. Adir straightened up and felt the sensation of self-compassion morph into relief. It was as if the colors of their surroundings were more vivid and crisp.

Give yourself a break.

Adir took a deep breath. He looked over at Brio, and when he spoke, every word was intentional. "What is my first step? What is *our* first step?"

"Let's rewind to earlier in this conversation. You'll begin to solve your problems when you recognize the dysfunction of opposition—of contradiction. Polar thinking between you and your partner leads to the misalignment and dissolution of your partnership—which is particularly bad because you two are two sides of the same coin. But if you're determined to be right above all, you will constantly struggle with any chance of alignment. Pivot from the reflexive desire to 'be right' to seeing the opportunities that rise when you let go."

Let go of being right.
Look for opportunities.

"But how?" Adir breathed the words, resigned while optimistic.

"Negative self-talk has aftershocks as devastating as an earthquake's. Following a traumatic event, your self-talk rumbles into your future, persisting unless you actively work to tamp it down.

"You must softly and gently replace the negative perceptions with this one redeeming thought: 'This is where we are. It's not where we'll stay.' Those simple words break the patterns that allow anxiety to infest your mind.

This is **where we are**.
It's not where we'll stay.

"Pursue complete acceptance. Keep pivoting to that soft voice. Keep letting go. When you can sit with the memory of your earthquake, and there's no charge, no negative buzz, you will finally be able to recover—and, even better, reinvent. You must accept in your bones that *disconnects in your thinking* work against you. When you let go of the fixation on being right, you open the door to collaborate with your powerful elephant."

Reinvention happens
when **memories** of the
earthquake are **benign**.

Adir needed to process this new information. Letting go wasn't part of his DNA, yet he was starting to realize that he'd had a "being right" blind spot that kept him from collaborating with Elgo.

The ant pulled out his notebook and scanned the conversation he just had. "Brio, thank you for your insights. There's a lot to unpack here. It kind of felt like criticism, but I get it."

"Adir, criticism is like manure. It stinks but helps you grow," the sage owl said with a chuckle.

"I'm going to write that down," said Adir as he drifted into the mental space of recounting all his lessons onto a blank page of his notebook.

Adir was so deep in thought that he didn't notice Brio leave. After a few minutes of writing in his Note-to-Self journal, he looked up and realized how little light was seeping through the vines.

"It must be the hour," thought Adir. He knew owls fed at night. As it was late, and others in the colony were settling in for a good night's sleep, Adir drifted off, knowing the next day was a day to take what he had learned and finally figure out how to align his intentions to flourish with his well-meaning elephant. Night would lead to a new day. Clearing skies promised a glorious sunrise from the east.

ADIR'S NOTES TO SELF

- Criticism is like manure. It stinks but helps me grow.
- A fixation on being right can be a blind-spot bias I don't even realize I have.
- After a setback, I have to get my subconscious mind right before I can drive toward my next goal.

- Silent suffering can become a habit. Some habits are absolutely not worth keeping.
- Pivot away from thoughts of disbelief to complete acceptance.
- Allow humility to chart my path of alignment with my partner.
- Give myself a break.
- Everyone, no matter how strong they are, experiences three stages as part of a devastating experience:
  — Stage 1: My Personal Earthquake
  — Stage 2: I Fight
  — Stage 3: My Post-traumatic Anxiety
- Let go of being right. Embrace ways to collaborate on "a new right" with my partner.
- This is where my elephant and I are. It's not where we'll stay.
- When I can sit with the memory of my earthquake, and there is no charge, no negative buzz, I will finally be able to reinvent.

CHAPTER 5

Learning the Hard Way

I will not stand for this!" howled Chromia. "We have the best pack in the Western Mountains. We have the best trackers from here to Black Rock Falls. It is unacceptable for us to have empty bellies and no sign of that elephant and its annoying ant. I have cubs to feed, as do all of you! We will not be denied. There must be an answer."

"I have an answer," came a raspy voice from the creature perched on the limb of a burned-out cedar tree that rose above the clearing.

Chromia's pack snapped their heads around to look up at a huge black mass framed by charred branches and silhouetted by a grey backdrop of clouds. The creature extended its neck, flapped its wings to shake off the mist they'd collected, and settled back onto the branch.

"Who are you?" asked Chromia.

"Valafar." He cleared his throat, though that had no discernable effect on his voice. "I am the son of King Verin. We have never formally met but we have enjoyed the meats of your labors. We clean the bones of your kills. We serve Mother Earth and all her wonderful ways."

"Valafar," said Chromia, eager to get to the point. "What solution do you have for our food situation? If we can't find a kill, you don't feed, either."

"Our methods may contrast, but our goals are the same. Good Chromia, you may govern the earth, but we rule the skies. We have two wings. You have four paws. You have piercing fangs, and we have curved beaks, both perfect for cutting into a fresh, thick carcass. Although we both see our prey, our perspectives differ. You use your victim's scent to bring them into view. We use the wind to carry us to heights from which our next meal comes into our sights. Our eyesight rivals that of our eagle brethren. Separately, wolves and vultures are dangerous for all who roam the earth, but together, we are deadly."

Sound rustled through the pack of wolves as they began to understand his proposition.

"This rain has left our hatchlings hungry. We need you to kill. You could use us to help with your kills. Plus, I despise Brio, that useless waste of feathers. The chance to know his friends took their last breath will make their rotting meat taste all the sweeter. Let us create a new option for filling our bellies. A real force of destruction. A killing team like no other," said Valafar.

In agitated agreement, the pack of wolves closed in on themselves. Chromia hushed the group in order to explain to Valafar her unsuccessful pursuit of Adir and Elgo. She described where they lost the scent of the duo. While she spoke, the rest of Valafar's flock joined them.

All the predators looked up, realizing the weather was breaking. Their chance to hunt was upon them.

Valafar and his kettle immediately flew east, headed toward the spot where Mill Creek and the eastern path intersected. Chromia assembled her pack and took off, but soon lost sight of the vultures above.

Chromia's nose led her on the trail, leaving her ego to direct her thoughts. She had a reputation to uphold and had been embarrassed when her pack realized she hadn't killed Adir and Elgo when she first encountered them. She had not only allowed them to escape that first time, but then completely leave the Oasis, evading her before she could make good on her promise to feast on their flesh.

Dusk turned to dark. The vultures hadn't been within their sights for hours. Chromia ordered the pack to assemble for the night. A new day would bring new promise for a kill they long hoped for. By morning, there was still no sign of Valafar and his flock. Chromia kept her wolves heading east on the open plains where any of the search vultures could easily spot their progress. By midafternoon, they rested while some of the pack were dubious they were chasing their meal in the proper direction. Chromia, sensing frustration, spurred her pack farther east. The uneven terrain forced them to zag past outcroppings of massive rock and zig through narrow openings in the high cliffs. In the waning light, Chromia's constant attention to the sky was rewarded as she caught sight of the vultures headed straight toward them.

Valafar fearlessly landed in front of Chromia while the rest of his kettle thought better than to trust a bunch of angry, hungry wolves. The vultures seemed tireless as they hung back a few dozen feet from the anxious pack.

"We are two days away from their hiding spot," cranked Valafar past his jagged vocal cords.

The wolves began to howl, which startled the vulture flock. Valafar didn't move. If anything, he leaned in. He stared at Chromia and took a fearless step forward.

"What do you say we set out at daybreak? We will fly overhead and I'll guide you to the location where they have set up their home. If we approach quietly, there would be no escape. They have the cover of vines but nowhere to retreat with the cliff at their backs. There is only one path in and one path out of the dense cactus that surrounds their spot. They would be trapped and your kill would be immediate."

As planned, they set out for two full and exhausting days of running. As promised, the vultures stayed with the pack, just slightly ahead and conscious that uneven terrain was different than as the vulture flies. By the end of the second day, Valafar confirmed they would be within striking distance of the base of the cliffs. An early-morning attack would catch the elephant, ant, and entire colony by surprise.

Just a few hundred feet from the overhanging vines and on the perimeter of the cactus field, Chromia ordered half her pack to round the expanse and enter into the other trail. There were only two entry and exit points that pointed directly at the curtain of vines. The wolves silently crept toward the ant and elephant's hideout. Shoulders of fur stealthily alternated into view above the level swath of prickly cacti. Valafar gave a signal from above as the sun breached the horizon on the east. In a scream of blood-thirsty howls, a dozen wolves exploded through the thick layer of hanging vines.

Despite the thick scent of an elephant and the remnants of a colony of creatures, the scene was deserted—nothing but dry dirt. Wolves snapped their exposed fangs left and right. Some immediately bounded out of the enclosure in chaos and confusion. Others tore up blankets of ferns and mounds of food scraps left behind. The place was infuriatingly vacated. The pack leered as they turned their focus on Chromia.

Their pack leader's eyes turned blood red and her teeth clenched tightly as she looked up each trail opening in the lost hope their prey was hiding nearby. Chromia shot her gaze upward at Valafar. The lead vulture nodded, torqued his feathered body, and shot eastward toward the plains. Despite the disappointment of a failed attack, the predators all knew they had to be close. The end of that elephant and ant was near.

As he had expected, the sunrise washed their Vine Spot camp in orange, warm light. Vestiges of that light sparkled through the dense foliage hanging around them. Adir was optimistic as he turned and looked at his notebook. "Today is going to be a great day," he said to Elgo as they both stretched and pushed the vines aside, allowing the morning's brilliance to immerse the muted enclosure.

Elgo saw the vultures before Adir did. In a fluid motion, the elephant retreated out of view and backed up to the cliff wall, while Adir peered through a small opening. The rising sun had warmed the earth enough to bubble up thermals of air that suspended a kettle of vultures, rotating upward in a frightening column of massive carrion eaters. Adir scanned the camp in front of him. They had carelessly left colony kids' toys lying about. He saw the lines and boxes of a hopscotch game they had made large enough for Elgo to play. It was clearly outlined, with round, deep elephant footprints in the dirt. He looked back up at the kettle of vultures, far above the cliff's edge. This instantly inspired the ant to call the colony into an emergency, hushed meeting.

"Wake up, everyone," Adir whispered. "We have a problem. A serious problem." Adir continued to explain what he suspected to be true. Vultures had found their hideout, and very well may alert others in the area that food, food known as "us," was nearby. "Who might the vultures tell? What if Chromia catches drift of what the vultures saw? If so, we are dead!" he thought to himself.

In turn, one member after the other looked up through slivers of openings in the vines. They witnessed the vultures catch a powerful thermal, high above their heads. "Look," said Adir. "They are leaving." As if shot out in the same rotational exit point, one winged marauder after the next headed back west toward the mountains.

"Gang, we're going to have to move. Vultures have spotted our camp. We are now in immediate danger. This could mean Chromia and her wolf pack may soon be headed our way." The choice was obvious. They had to leave. The colony feverishly began to collect their belongings.

A couple of hours later, they pushed aside the vines, rushed past the hopscotch game to the cactus thicket's edge. They were again poised for a journey of uncertainty. At the trailhead, Adir, on the back of Elgo, turned and announced in an even tone, "Sometimes, the hard way is the only way. Let's move." Adir noticed his anxiety was replaced by the task at hand. Now that he had immediate survival to focus on, he was inspired to get back in the fight and Take Action. He double-checked for his notepad that was now wrapped in rainproof palm leaf. He ensured it was tucked securely in a skinfold behind Elgo's ear. Although the notepad was important to him, now was the time for survival. Introspection became a distant thought. From the serrated peaks behind them, thunder growled.

Later that day, and the next, spring showers followed more rain with impending downpours on the horizon. Dark, crowded clouds now hung low in the sky. The miserable weather infested their mood. Adir, Elgo, and their fellow travelers grumbled and trudged as they moved north toward a broken sign that pointed toward the Splitnit River crossing. Although the winter season was behind them, nothing braved the elements to pop out of the earth. Ground color could have added life to their journey. Instead, a dull brownish-grey landscape blended with featureless skies. And, as Adir and Elgo grew hungrier, they became more aware that the predators who might be stalking them were also ravenous.

Back at their former camp, more than one storm brewed.

Chromia could feel her pack questioning her leadership skills the second they caught on to this additional mistake she'd made in their attempts to eat Adir and Elgo. She had no intention of being a lone wolf. She knew her status was in question. Standing in front of the vacated Vine Spot hideout, with wolves anxiously sniffing around a cold camp, Chromia was determined to prove to her pack that she was worthy as their Alpha Wolf.

As an Alpha Wolf, she reveled in the respect she got from her pack. They looked to her for answers and leadership. She enjoyed the deference her fellow wolves afforded her. If a young wolf got out of hand, she only had to bare her fangs and growl to keep them in line. Honestly, much of her self-worth came from controlling the pack. So while the older wolves attempted to guide her leadership style, she remained her own wolf. *Rule with strength and conviction* was her motto.

She dismissed her elders' advice when they said, "Suffering and misery come from ego. Fulfillment and bliss come from letting go." She convinced herself they were old and out of touch, refusing to let go of her pride.

Suffering and misery
come from ego.
Fulfillment and bliss come
from letting go.

"This way," yelped Chromia, and the pack eagerly followed her north.

For miles, they kept following the elephant tracks, covering ground that would be ten times faster than a plodding elephant could travel. The scent increased in strength as it inspired the pack to run faster.

The tracks ended in a creek. Instinctively, Chromia looked up to locate the vultures, hoping that their position would reveal a clue. A couple of miles off, directly northeast, Chromia spotted Valafar and his kettle circling.

Chromia's revenge was mere minutes away. She gathered her pack. "Do you smell that?" she yelped. "That is the smell of elephant blood!"

The pack howled in anticipation.

"Follow me, good wolves. Dinner is about to be served."

She broke through the ranks and pounded new tracks over the muddy banks of the creek. The splash of sludge and muck splattered Chromia's fur while a deluge of mud flung airborne onto each wolf following her lead. As Chromia led the pack toward the clearing, she picked up the pace. Thoughts of regaining her pride and filling her belly with fresh elephant meat consumed her.

A couple of miles ahead of the bloodthirsty wolf pack, the rain had subsided, allowing Adir and Elgo to organize their group for a river crossing. While they didn't know how safe they were, their instincts had them marshaling an urgent and efficient crossing of the river in front of them. The modest-sized ferry would take them across Splitnit River by a raft-pulley system, but with Elgo's size, they would need two trips. So Adir and Elgo sent the colony ahead first.

The moment the raft touched the opposite shore, a sickening sound snatched their attention. A thousand feet behind Adir and

Elgo were seventeen wet and glistening wolves barreling down the slope of loose river rock. Only then, as they looked up at the onslaught from the ridge, did Adir and Elgo notice a dozen vultures circling above.

Adir and Elgo immediately started yanking on the pulley. "Hurry!" yelled Adir. The last of the colony finally jumped onto shore on the northern side of the river, their panicked screams making it all too obvious how dire this situation was. The raft twisted and turned as it fought the current.

"HURRY!" screamed Adir.

The wolves were five hundred feet away.

Four hundred feet.

Three hundred feet.

"There's no time, Elgo. We have to grab on to the rope and pull ourselves across. Now. Now! NOW!" The wolves were two hundred feet away.

By the time the wolves were only one hundred feet away, Adir and Elgo had started their cross, Elgo grasping the rope with his trunk, Adir riding on his back—then his head, then the tip of his brow as the water grew deeper—trying desperately to cross the river. While Elgo was straining against the current that was pulling them under, Adir was desperate to hang on as he was buffeted by blasts of water from all directions.

Elgo would not let go, the end of his trunk tipped toward the sky so he could breathe no matter how tumultuous the water became. Adir scurried up an elephant hair to avoid being submerged.

Elgo placed one foot in front of the next as all twenty thousand pounds of him combined with the force of the water to stretch the rope to capacity.

Then their progress stopped. The rope slacked, jerked, then cinched a knot around Elgo's trunk. Suddenly, they were headed in the opposite direction; Elgo lost his footing as the wolves worked in unison to tug the rope—with the elephant and ant attached to it—back to the gallows side of the shore. They used the pulley system, their powerful jaws and muscular bodies flexing to pull their victims back to shore.

Adir tried to yell, "LET GO!" but he choked on water. Elgo was helpless in straining his footing on the slippery river floor. Seventeen formidable, angry, and ravenous wolves were having their way.

Then the vultures joined in the attack, each one folding its wings, in turn, to dive at Adir and Elgo's exposed trunk, ears, and eyes. Adir got knocked into the water and went under. He thrashed all six appendages in an attempt to clasp any part of Elgo's body. He was barely able to hang on.

Elgo was rapidly being yanked toward the southern shore. Adir was losing all hope.

Chromia, filled with pride, leaped to the edge of the shore and focused her blue and brown eyes directly at Adir, who had just surfaced.

"Did I not make myself clear?" growled Chromia. "I. Never. Let. G—"

There was an earsplitting SNAP. Elgo's weight, the relentless current, and the wolves' sharp fangs, when combined, were too much for the rope to endure. The cord ruptured at its weakest point, in contact with Elgo's trunk, the recoil forming a sharp whip that lashed Chromia's side. She shrieked in agony.

Adir and Elgo were swept into the southern, treacherous fork in Splitnit River, where rocks and rapids seized the terrain. Cliffs and rocky outcroppings menaced over either side of the unrelenting current. Elgo's musculature and the torrent from the rapids kept him down, with all but the tip of his trunk underwater. Adir clambered to reach that endpoint to also breathe. Within seconds, they were out of view of both their horrified colony and the maelstrom of hungry vultures. The wolf pack turned to attend to Chromia's bloody injury. Tracing Elgo and Adir, now lost down the river, was no longer the pack's concern.

But Adir and Elgo were not safe. In fact, they continued to be in peril. The uncompromising rapids gained speed and power as the water shallowed from twenty feet deep to just ten and sometimes six feet. Elgo was no match for the powerful torrents bouncing them from rock to craggy rock. It was futile to fight the current south and east in the opposite direction of where the colony was to travel. Each time Elgo attempted to swim or crawl to the edge, the unrelenting flow would push them deeper into both the river and exhaustion. The river was nonnegotiable. It would determine their fate.

Consequently, they adapted. When they could float, they caught their breath. Elgo learned to pivot his feet downstream and spring sideways off barbed rocks rather than being dashed and lacerated against them.

After over two hours of pounding and bouncing in the icy water, they eventually came to rest at a forgiving eddy, realizing that they had survived only by letting go of any sense of control.

Dusk gave way to the pitch dark of an overcast night.

In the still and total darkness, Adir thought about his tendency to fight for a solution. This time, nature had clearly wagged its finger at his plans to escape the force of the frigid water.

"Make all the plans you want," he imagined Mother Nature whispering in the wind above. "One day you'll learn to bend with the oncoming force, rather than fight it."

Bend with the oncoming force, rather than fight it.

It began to rain again, then pour, then a deluge fell from the heavens. They shivered too badly to sleep.

The concept of collaboration would not leave Adir's thoughts as he lay miserably awake. Being swept into the violent current was a lesson in adapting, in collaborating with the flow. In addition to bending with the oncoming force, he made a mental note to add collaborating with the flow in his notepad.

Collaborate with the flow.
Adapt.

But for now, it was simply the coldest, longest, darkest night of their lives.

The next morning, rain continued to drench their spirits as they took their only option: skirting along the river's edge looking for a trail to climb out of the gorge. Hungry and numb from losing their colony, they trudged forward looking for a way up and out. One day morphed into the next as hope on an ascending trail led back to the river's edge. With each hope for progress, the jagged contour of the crevasse led them to a sheer cliff with no chance to rise higher. There seemed to be no end to a frustrating upstream return to the banks of smooth river rock.

It took another week in the Splitnit Gorge for them to find a way to climb out of the deep ravine. On the eighth day of being separated from their colony, while it continued to rain, they finally found worn switchbacks that tested Elgo's footing on a slippery ascension. Once above Splitnit Gorge, an expansive plateau that was framed on the northern border horizon by a snowy ridge of peaks spread out before them. The unassailable elevation to the north dictated their only traveling option: south and east.

After a few hours of low clouds and laboring through sloppy ground, they found a grove of banana trees. As they gorged on the delicious fruit, Elgo leaned up against a tree for cover from the continuing rainfall. He peeked over at Adir as the ant patted him on the leg. "Elgo, I don't know how, but we're still alive, and we still have hope. Maybe there is a reason for all this hardship," said Adir as he looked at their surroundings. He was finally able to pull out his writing pad and catch up on his notes. Writing his thoughts always buoyed his spirits.

By the next morning, the rain had stopped. The sun returned. They headed farther south to find an elevated table of rock that looked out over the land. As they perched on the edge, Brio showed up.

Brio reassured Adir and Elgo, informing them that their colony was okay, but roughly five hundred miles north. They filled Brio in on their side of the vulture-wolf attack, and their trials down the Splitnit Gorge. Together, the trio hatched a plan to reunite with the colony by journeying to where the Splitnit ultimately fed into the harbor. It was a circuitous path but it gave them hope.

"In the meantime, we have some work to do—did you notice the contradiction in your recent struggle?"

"Brio," said Adir in a joking tone, "can we give the lessons a rest just for a day?"

"Ha! Listen, creatures who never worked in tandem decided to team up: the wolves and vultures collaborated in an innovative attempt to bring you to an early demise. They worked on what became an entirely new option for them. For the first time, they worked together. Though they failed this time, next attempt they may succeed. You must learn from this experience in order to go from surviving to thriving." Brio sounded thrilled.

Adir and Elgo nodded in resigned disbelief, not quite sure why Brio was excited about a lesson regarding them nearly being eaten.

"The rulers of the air and earth looked past their contradiction and found common ground to make them even more powerful. Tomorrow, it's your turn."

Adir was too exhausted to give in to his curiosity and ask Brio what he meant by that, so they turned and watched the sun set below the western horizon. From their high vantage, the tips of the Western Range were barely visible, but what they could see created a jagged horizon accentuated by deep yellow and orange, making for a glorious sunset. It was a sunset that promised that tomorrow would be a new day of growth and renewed hope.

Adir thought back to the moment they left the vulnerable Vine Spot. He remembered how he had announced to his friends, *Sometimes the hard way is the only way.* He clarified his thoughts out loud. "Elgo, sometimes the hard way is the only way we will learn."

Sometimes the **hard way**
is the only way we will learn.

ADIR'S NOTES TO SELF

- Suffering and misery come from ego. Fulfillment and bliss come from letting go.
- Bend with the oncoming force rather than fighting it.
- Sometimes the hard way is the only way we will learn.
- Collaborate with the flow. Adapt.

Chapter 6

Rebound and Redefine

S taring south, the Mudflats lay as far as they could see. Adir and Elgo had only one option: south. If they turned north or east, they would be trapped either by the wall of high plains or the river gorge. If they turned west, they would be taking themselves farther away from finding their friends and family. Despite the immensity of the challenge, the Mudflats awaited their first step.

It would be up to Elgo to muscle through the landscape while Adir observed from the relative comfort of Elgo's back.

While there was plenty of sunshine, it quickly became clear to Adir how the Mudflats got their name. It was a basin of mud, moss, and low-lying shrubs. Despite the sunlight flooding the landscape, days of unrelenting rain combined with ample shade from miles of bushes would result in one hard slog. Elgo, with renewed energy from the sunny days and banana groves along their trek, ventured forward.

Each step seemed harder than the last. They desperately searched for an easier way, but while mossy high points had less mud, they were covered with unforgiving clusters of shrubs.

Adir knew that innovation could save the day, so he convinced Brio to help him fashion shin guards out of a collection of smooth sticks lying around the shrubs. With roots yanked out of the ground, they wrapped and secured the wood protections on Elgo's front legs. In theory, if Elgo's legs were defended, they could crash through the dense brush, zigzagging their way from high point to high point across the Mudflats. Instead, the combination of slippery moss, jagged barbs of shrubbery, and the thickness of the unrelenting growth left Elgo floundering, slipping, falling, and bloodily scratching himself as they slipped back into the muddy base.

But Adir didn't give up his curious ways. He kept his ideas coming.

Next, they tried fabricating snowshoes that would work on the mud. They ended up being woven saucers on the bottom of Elgo's feet. Only two steps in and Adir's creative solution was another crappy failure. But still, Adir refused to give up on finding an answer.

"Maybe if we break off dead branches, we can make a path along the top of the mud?" Adir's curiosity only led to more frustration for Elgo.

But after a half-day of failed experiments, Adir ran out of ideas and the sticky truth set in.

"Straight through the middle is the only way," he admitted. What lay in front of them seemed endless. Going straight ahead felt like the ultimate uncertainty. "What if we never get out of this?" Adir thought with a long exhale. Elgo picked up what his ant was unintentionally putting down. Marching into impending struggle was counterintuitive and against Elgo's nature. Adir had to literally talk himself and his elephant into the next step, and the next. This self-talk never got easier. There was no momentum to be had. Each move forward was absolute, joyless labor.

By midday, Elgo was drained of energy. Ten steps and he had to rest. Ten more steps and he was gasping for air. Eventually, nine-step increments turned into eight. By late afternoon, taking only three steps between breaks, they looked back. They were still depressingly close to where they'd entered the swampy Mudflats.

Elgo leaned up against a mound of moss and shrubs, hanging his head. He had no more strength left to give and Adir knew it.

Brio looked on, wondering what Adir's next move would be.

"Elgo, we tried my ideas. Nothing brought us any closer to a solution. The disc shoes seemed better suited for getting sucked into mud than walking across it. Heck, laying down a path of broken sticks would only have worked if we had twenty more years to get through this quagmire. The shin guards idea was a joke. So here we are. In the unadulterated pit of stuckness. We can't go back because there's still no other way back to our friends and family, but we can't go forward, either. Not without—without what? What am I possibly missing?" cried Adir, not knowing where the inspiration to dig deeper would come from.

All around them, finches flitted about. Squirrels wove their way from branch to branch. Adir watched them, wondering what kept them so busy. He studied a particularly industrious squirrel who gathered dried and dead moss that it had snatched up. He watched the squirrel load up on his bounty then scurry into the middle of the tallest scrub. What he couldn't see before became clearly visible now. It was a nest. The squirrel was taking care of her family.

To the right, Adir noticed another nest hidden under a canopy of leaves. A couple of male and female finches were visiting their own nest. In one of their beaks, a worm squirmed and contorted as it disappeared past the upper rim of the nest and out of view. Adir angled his head to hear chirping from baby birds.

"I wonder what our colony is doing right now?"

Elgo's head still hung low, as he resigned himself to the futile nature of their situation.

"I wonder if they are setting up camp somewhere north?"

Elgo flapped an ear and lifted his gaze.

"I wonder how far they've traveled? Could they be farther east in a warmer climate? Can you imagine them waiting for us beside the river somewhere?"

Elgo took a deep breath. He lifted his head and replaced his frown with the lilt of a smile. Talking about family was lifting his spirits. He started to hum a deep sound of confidence and promise. Adir dashed up the bridge of Elgo's brow and pointed to what looked like an elevated section. "Maybe the mud is only a foot deep in that section over there."

Adir lay facedown on Elgo's head and said, "Our colony needs us, my friend. We belong with family, and they belong with us."

Elgo nodded as his thoughts of family elevated his focus. He lifted his right front leg and his back left leg while leaning in the direction Adir was pointing. "We got this, Elgo. We got this."

Elgo took a step.

Then another.

Deeper they marched, into the bog, one deliberate step after the other.

An elephant's mind is complex. It can experience hope and despair at the same time—which is exactly what was happening with Elgo. While the motivation to reunite with the colony drove him forward with every step, the Mudflats were a physical reminder that life was hard. Struggle is the way it is (and will always be!). He found himself repeatedly thinking that he, Adir, and the colony might be better off at the Vine Spot. They were safe there. Life was simple. Especially because there was no mud.

The sun beat down on them with relentless ferocity while the ground didn't seem any closer to drying out. By dusk, Elgo was spent. Covered in muck that turned into heavy, muddy weights around his ankles, with dried, thick splotches on his back, Elgo was truly a hot mess.

Elgo plopped down on a moist pad of thick moss and immediately fell asleep without the energy to eat.

The next morning, Elgo was famished. He ate the leaves off every shrub within twenty feet. But as they got moving, the sludge was at least as thick, if not thicker, than it had been the day before. Each step down made a *squishing* sound that alternated with a flatulent, sucking sound that rang out every time Elgo attempted to remove a foot from where he'd placed it and take the next step. After ten steps, he had to rest for a few seconds.

Ten more steps.

Another breather.

Elgo had a pounding headache, so Adir encouraged him to drink more along the way. The pools of sludge water seemed revolting. Still, he had no choice.

The second day progressed—or rather, devolved, to Elgo's way of thinking. With zero energy, he smacked down onto another small patch of a mossy bed. The elephant immediately slipped into a fitful slumber.

Day three was excruciating. Elgo needed extraordinary encouragement. He was destitute. Each pause to rest was longer than the prior one. While Adir and Brio could see a rise in the landscape ahead—a rise that indicated the end of the muddy bog and this agonizing journey—Elgo never saw it. He never looked up to see it. He felt feeble and helpless. No matter what Adir told him, he didn't take it in. It should have taken two hours to reach the dry, raised ground, to finally get higher and drier. The slog to the very end of the bog took the balance of the day.

They arrived on dry ground after dark. Elgo plopped down, legs splayed, trunk flopped out in front of him, the picture of elephantine exhaustion.

Adir was concerned, and Brio recognized the severity of the situation. The owl, sensitive to the prospect of a teaching moment during trying times, wanted to ensure the lessons would continue. Brio never bought into the "break you down to build you up" approach to learning. The best time to infuse any insights would be after a good night's sleep. To prime the learning pump, the wise owl opted to plant some ideas that would germinate in their slumber.

"I'm so excited!" blurted out Brio.

Adir lifted his head. Elgo managed to lift open one eyelid.

"It is at times of discomfort when we learn the most! Yes, it's hard. Yes, your situation seemed hopeless. But the challenge is behind us and a lesson is in front of us."

Elgo looked up at Adir, searching for any reason to be excited. Adir nodded and said, "We're exhausted and can't even imagine moving forward. Yet, you seem convinced. Whatcha got?" The question hung in the air, paying homage to the befuddlement of the ant and the elephant at the attitude of the owl.

"Listen, you two. It's in the depths of hopelessness that the seeds of a new beginning appear. Sleep on how your differences impeded your progress. The toil you just experienced may lead to the traction necessary to escape being stuck ever again."

Our differences must not impede our progress.

Adir and Elgo were too spent to fully digest Brio's lesson, but he had never steered them wrong. "Listen," said Brio, "just sleep on four words. 'Differences lead to progress.' In the morning we'll see what percolated in your minds."

They eventually wished the owl a good night. "Differences . . . ," muttered Adir. Within seconds, Elgo and Adir were both asleep.

The next day, as finches flitted from branch to shrub and back, Adir woke in a somewhat startled state of disorientation. The tired pair eased into a realization and gratefulness that the Mud-flats were behind them. Brio was comfortably sitting beside them while holding a leaf in his left claw.

"What's that?" asked Adir while stretching.

"When I was thinking about the concept of differences, I wrote a poem. I wanted to explain the source of why many of us struggle to accomplish anything in the first place. What is it about contradictions that stands in our way of getting unstuck?" queried Brio. "Would you like to read it? Maybe read it aloud for Elgo to take it in?"

Adir rubbed his eyes, cleared his throat, and read the verse so that Brio and Elgo could hear every word.

Under the heavens, people recognize beauty because ugly exists.
When people see something as good, they know evil persists.
The tangible and intangible produce one another.
Difficult and easy sit across from each other.

Long and short can explain a state.
High and low, two sides of a plate.
Before and after are like links on some chains.
As night follows day, the light surely wanes.

The Sage acts by doing nothing
And silently conveys purposed thinking.
His lessons arise and yet they fall;
He creates, then he lets go of it all.

He is rich but holds not a penny,
He has intention, but expectation? Not any.
When his work is complete, he takes no praise.
His canvas is painted bringing clarity to the haze.

That is why it will last forever.

Brio alternated from one set of talons to the next impatiently and finally asked, "What does that make you think of?"

Adir looked back at the entire verse, scratched his chin, then said, "I can see how differences interact. How contradictions and things that aren't like the other coexist."

"You're on the right track," replied Brio, nodding and continuing to rock from leg to leg. "The poem is also about our perception of contradictions. There is contrast of the mind and the body. There is a polarity between positive and negative, awake and asleep, idealism and realism, subjective and objective, wealth and poverty, happy and unhappy, even day and night."

"Huh?" Adir was confused.

"As you know, contradictions are everywhere. But think of contradictions as a cocreating relationship between two entities. Imagine each entity had an opinion—if Positive was a person who always thought he was both right and more important than his conjoined partner, Negative. Or if Idealism was convinced that its way was superior to Realism. Or Subjective thought the same of Objective. And imagine if Unhappy just knew it took precedence over Happy, and no one could tell Unhappy any different."

Brio's personification of the concepts helped Adir understand their relationship. He started to grasp the disconnect that would result from such a dynamic. After all, if the two sides of one coin each thought they were not only better than but could exist without the other side, then the coin itself would . . . well, Adir didn't know exactly what would happen, but there would be chaos.

"It's only by accepting both sides of something that you find harmony, since neither can exist without the other. Differences set you up for harmony by enabling coexistence. And isn't harmony the best option?" Brio continued on without needing an answer. "Problems start when one side thinks it's more important than the other or attempts to take priority. Remember in the Vine Spot where you were determined to be right and have Elgo do things your way? That's exactly what I'm saying not to do. When there is balance, both of you are 'right' at the same time. There is harmony."

Problems start when one
side predominates.

"Other than being clear that breakfast time is turning into lunchtime, I'm still not 100 percent clear on what you're getting at," said Adir, nudging for an example.

"Let's say the sun and the moon had an argument about who was more important.* The sun says, 'I light up the day. I warm the earth and all things grow with my loving energy. Therefore, I am more important.' Then the moon says, 'Not so. I remind all the creatures to rest and restore for the day ahead. I keep the tides

---

* Now you have a problem? The sun arguing with a moon is not believable? You've gone this far believing an ant and an owl have regular conversations. But you're not buying celestial conversations? Carry on.

in sync and the world in balance. I am more important.' Imagine the chaos if the sun or the moon were adamant about being right, while ignoring the other's point of view—what if one decided to simply not relinquish their territory to the other? Wouldn't the world literally stop turning?

"So to avoid that, they let go of the need for dominance. They must agree they are both important and form a unique synergy that enables the world to turn. They—and everything they influence—are better off when they blend solutions together."

"So what you're saying is the harmony in contradiction is part of the world order?" Adir said. "Chromia and Valafar lived for generations like their ways were the *right* way, but they found a better solution for them—a more creative way to align. Your examples—awake and asleep? Both work in tandem. Or when there is an objective position, there must be a subjective opinion. Or happy puts unhappy in perspective. Without pain, we'd never know the value of pleasure. That's what you're getting at, right?"

"Precisely. That's the polar nature of duality, which is the way to understand the nature of balance and alignment. Now, relate that to the personal aftershocks you've experienced since the earthquake. Think about our discussions on resonating with your elephant. It can feel like Mudflats of the mind. Endless struggle. Exhausting challenges. Hopeless effort. The quintessential feeling of being stuck."

"Wait a second. Did you take us through that field to teach us a lesson?"

"No, my little six- and four-legged friends. Do you know the saying 'When the student is ready, the teacher will appear'? In the spirit of that: 'Live the lesson to learn the lesson.'"

Live the lesson
to learn the lesson.

"True. The Mudflats was the only way we could travel. And, indeed, to learn what we needed to learn."

Brio continued, happy to see them internalize the lesson. "You've been learning about the way to a solution over this past year or so. Since the earthquake, you've been grappling with the ways your thinking contradicts Elgo's natural tendencies. The truth is, you've put too much importance on being right. Remember how you didn't want to let go of your point of view in the Vine Spot? Think of how detrimental the need to be right all the time was to your ant and elephant relationship. You are living through the traumatic stages of your personal earthquake—the fight just to survive, the powerful forces of anxiety and panic. You never gave up during these terrible days in the Mudflats.

"In other words, you have experienced the power of the Solution Loop."

"The What Loop?" Adir said, scratching his head.

"The Solution Loop. It is a sequence of phases that, if you follow them, will enable you and Elgo to finally escape the feeling of being stuck. You have already unknowingly experienced the six phases. Now you're ready to explore how to make them work for you. Follow this sequential loop and you will be able to test solutions until you find one that gets you unstuck."

Brio pulled out two maple leaves and opened them up. Lying flat was a rare six-petal plumeria flower. Each petal had words inscribed on it. The flower was preserved with a clear, thin, hardened resin. The end of the stem had a hole in it. Brio laid it at Adir's feet.

"Look at this sequence as phases of what you have experienced since the earthquake. As best you can, describe it to Elgo. A collection of these phases is the way for both of you to escape any future version of a mudflat like the one you just found yourselves in. These mudflats of the mind are not dissimilar to the helpless, stuck feeling you had at the Oasis after the earthquake, or the stuck sensation you experienced at the Vine Spot, or even the one you felt during that brief encounter at the banks of the Split-nit River when the wolves were attacking you. For any challenges you've had, or the ones you will have, the Solution Loop is your eventual way out."

Adir thought about how, in each situation, he had felt helpless and stuck. Brio's words piqued his curiosity.

Adir looked at the flower.

The topmost of the plumeria petals said, "Grasp the Contradiction."

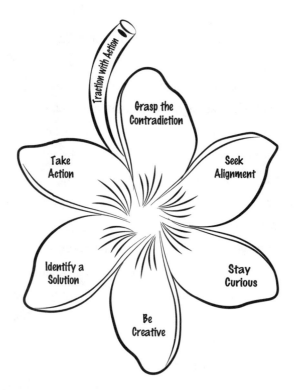

Brio continued as Adir studied the flower. "In life we find ourselves in the contradiction in many relationships. Not just the obvious ones between someone and a spouse, or you and a relative, or with coworkers, or with neighbors, but also relationships between you and nature. There was even a contradiction in the Mudflats between what the Mudflats dictated and what Elgo would rather do. But the most important contradiction at hand is between you and your elephant. There is a lack of acceptance of the difference between you and Elgo that we need to examine. Think about it this way:

"While you want to *make* things happen, Elgo wants things to just happen.

"You want to do while Elgo wants to be.

"You want to act as Elgo is determined to feel.

"You want to explore, but Elgo wants to stay put.

"You want to take risks, yet Elgo wants to be safe.

"You want to grow though Elgo wants to simplify.

"You want to go forward into the adventure. Elgo wants to retreat back to the known.

"And until you embrace the fact that there will always be two sides to everything, you won't be able to ultimately align and work toward a solution. Once you Grasp the Contradiction, you will be on your way to finding a solution that you can both agree and, especially, act upon."

Adir instantly saw the truth in their contradiction and knew Elgo could feel it, too. Armed with this new reality, they had the potential for aligning their decisions and efforts.

"So what's our solution?" asked Adir, gesturing to his silent friend.

"That is for you both to land on." Brio used the hole on the stem of the Solution Loop plumeria on an elephant hair at the crest of Elgo's head. The emblem glistened with promise in the light of day.

Adir looked at the plumeria petals and imagined what each one meant to him. When it came to the petal that said "Grasp the Contradiction," he mused out loud, "Brio, I might need to admit that sticking in my heels is a mistake. What if I'm causing the disconnect in our thinking?" Adir felt a little rumble under his feet. This was a sure sign that Elgo was resonating with what his ant just mentioned. Adir made a mental note to be aware of any disconnect that may occur with him and his powerful partner.

Adir paused to ruminate on the next petal, which said, "Seek Alignment." He scanned back to Brio's admonition that Adir let go of "being right." The ant wondered out loud, "Brio, as you've pointed out, I have a habit, or fixation even, on 'being right.' I get how I need to let go of that. But does an elephant that is driven by instinct and emotion let go of being right?"

"This is a great question, and a lifelong question that has no immediate answer," responded Brio. "Like dealing with the forces of nature, or an environment you have no control over, you may have to work with what you've got. Instinct and emotion are automatic, habitual, pattern responses by Elgo. It is only over time that you can methodically shift any old habits that are established today but have the possibility of changing in your tomorrows."

"I hear ya," said Adir. "At least I can open the door for aligning with my elephant." Again, with Elgo feeling what Adir was thinking, there were the beginnings of another shudder. "An elephant buzz is always worth paying attention to. I'll keep finding ways to let go of being right, and we can keep seeking alignment," he acknowledged to Elgo. The tremble under Adir correlated to a significant tingle up and down his own tiny back. It was absolutely a calibration of deep unity that letting go of "being right" was indeed important.

Adir directed his focus back at the next two petals: "Then, Stay Curious in Order to Be Creative." He glanced up at Brio for a response. The owl smiled and nodded as if to say, "Go on."

"Okay, curious and creative. I guess we look for ideas that could work."

"Tell me more, Adir," encouraged Brio. "What are some examples since the earthquake where you stayed curious and maintained your creativity?"

"We just experienced this in the Mudflats. We tried zigging and zagging from mossy mound to mossy mound. We tried the snowshoes. Turns out, there is a very good reason they don't call them 'mud shoes.' And, admittedly, the broken sticks path was a good idea in theory but way, way, waaaaaaay too time consuming to be practical. So, yes, we were curious and creative. But heck, Brio," said Adir, interrupting himself, "I can't say I'm the most patient of ants, and I can easily get frustrated. Even though I was trying to keep up a positive voice for my elephant, I was terribly frustrated. This can't be good for Elgo as he's doing the best an elephant can do."

"Adir, you bring up an important point. Frustration leads to doubts, and this is poison for Elgo's thoughts."

"So I'm just supposed to pretend to be positive and have no doubts?" Adir implored for an answer.

"Allow me to quote Willi-Ant Shakespeare. 'Therein lies the rub.' Focusing on the setbacks is where the problem is and where the solution awaits. It takes more than discipline to be positive. You must embrace your affinity for learning through curiosity and creativity. Frustration comes from failure. But embrace failure as growth. If you change your mind to learning what works, you will Stay Curious and Be Creative. It's a simple shift to learning over all else. Adir, you love to learn. Everyone loves to learn. Seize that instinct. Put yourself in the mode of: 'How about this? No? Then how about that? No? How about something different? Or this option? Or that option?' Your awareness grows with each attempt. In the Mudflats, you learned what didn't work and resolved to keep moving. Put the words *resolute* and *solution* together and you have *resolution*. Stay Curious and Be Creative and you are then ready to Identify a Solution."

"Identify a Solution," he said while letting the two words hang in the air like the fresh smell of rain. "Hmm, I like how that feels!" continued Adir, taking in the concept while noting its familiarity.

"What does 'Identify a Solution' mean to you, Adir?"

"I like finding solutions. The fact is, I'd rather skip all the other phases and go directly to a solution."

"Is that possible after an earthquake?" asked Brio.

Adir stiffened. He was instantly taken back to how he had stubbornly tried to rebuild in the earthquake zone of the compromised Oasis. He realized how his frustration in the Vine Spot was due to his inability to conjure up a better solution than their hand-to-mouth existence. He reminded himself of the futility of any solution at all in the Splitnit Gorge or the Mudflats.

"No," said Adir after his moment of reflection. "But how can you find a solution that works?" he asked.

"In the Solution Loop, you're not asked to FIND a solution. You're asked to Identify a Solution that may work," said Brio as he pointed at the stem of the plumeria. "You will only know if your possible solution worked after you've taken action on it. Action that has viable traction will extract you out of the loop of 'Does this work? Does this work? Does this work?' It's easier to imagine that you can escape stuckness of an earthquake's devastation by just stepping out of the setback. But that's not how it works. Remember how we said there's no linear way out of chaos?"

"Yes," said Adir while Elgo was taking it all in.

"The Solution Loop is designed to be a tool for learning as you go into the middle of the unknown.

"These are not steps on a linear path. The phases of grasping the contradiction, seeking alignment by letting go, and staying curious with a broad focus circulate until they get traction. It can take months, if not years, for this sequence to cycle, and re-cycle, you out of stuckness. To truly put your personal earthquake behind you, be patient with this process. Much as you wouldn't pull a flower to make it grow faster, don't force your way ahead until you both agree to go to the next petal. If your solution activity works, you'll recognize the traction quite quickly. You will have broken ground from the sticky, gooey, mucky nature of the metaphorical Mudflats into a new life. I've inscribed each element of this sequence on a plumeria to remind you that ideas blossom into a colorful future that awaits. Got it?"

You wouldn't **pull** a flower
to make it **grow faster**.
In the same way,
don't **force** the solution.

"I like this!" replied Adir optimistically. Elgo reverberated his agreement.

"Because getting 'unstuck' is the treasure you seek, allow me to summarize the Solution Loop in a fun way. Let's make sure this Solution Loop sinks in for both you and Elgo. Since the Maswali Forest stands directly between you and a reunion with your colony, I'm going to advance you through a series of tests. Pass each level on this quest and you will be able to bring a deeper understanding of the Solution Loop sequence. Have you ever experienced a treasure hunt game where one clue leads you to the next?"

Adir answered, "We've done this with the colony kids, but I've never been on a grown-up version."

"I'll make it fun. Each clue will lead you through the forest. When you fully understand each insight, you'll be ready to internalize the next. I'd like this treasure hunt to help you contextualize all the lessons you've endured and the challenges you've superseded. Your treasure will be the actions that truly have the traction necessary to escape stuckness. Give me a head start and I'll create the progression for you. Rest here and set out in the morning. I need a bit of time to set this all up." Brio smiled, winked, and finished with, "See ya, boys—the Solution Loop awaits!" As he flapped off, disappearing into the forest, Brio could be heard saying, "Remember, don't force it. Take the time you neeeeeeeeeed."

"It looks like we're going into the woods," Adir said, curious to learn Brio's summary of their lessons from the earthquake and the personal aftershocks that had shaken their lives since then.

As Adir pulled out his notepad to jot down a few breakthrough ideas, he could tell his elephant wasn't thrilled by another uncertain foray into the unknown. "Listen, Elgo, we got this. We'll make it fun, and we will figure out this flower thing. Let's just follow Brio's directions and admire that cute little plumeria in the middle of your forehead."

Elgo didn't respond. He was not amused.

Unfazed, Adir spent the balance of the waning hour of sunlight adding to and reviewing his Notes to Self.

ADIR'S NOTES TO SELF

- Our differences must not impede our progress.
- Problems start when one side predominates.
- Live the lesson to learn the lesson.
- Learn the phases of the Solution Loop:
  - Grasp the Contradiction.
  - Seek Alignment.
  - Stay Curious
  - Be Creative
  - Identify a Solution
  - Take Action
- I wouldn't pull a flower to make it grow faster. In the same way, I won't force the solution.

CHAPTER 7

The Solution Loop Treasure

The Maswali Forest was a unique woodland. Its majestic baobabs were exceptionally tall, thick trees with a colossal, umbrellalike canopy. It was a peaceful and daunting place where all who entered were reminded of who lorded over the land: the baobabs. All living things that wander into the Maswali Forest are immediately struck by how tiny they are among the gargantuan trees. While Adir was used to being dwarfed by the expanse and creatures around him, this was a first for Elgo. As he stepped foot onto the grassy forest floor, the baobab trees made him feel like an insignificant weed.

Brio's promise of a treasure hunt became immediately evident when they were just a few hundred feet into the grove. Pinned to a goliath tree, at eye level for an ant riding on the back of an elephant, was a note. Upon closer scrutiny, it revealed three words: "The First Phase."

The First Phase sat on a small stack of discarded baobab leaves, an invitation. Elgo gingerly grasped the parchment with the end of his trunk, depositing it in the space beside the plumeria petals' Solution Loop.

Adir reached down and recognized Brio's handwriting. He carefully read out loud, so that they could interpret the message together. "The First Phase. Grasp the Contradiction. Welcome the differences between your and Elgo's ways of thinking. Every breakdown will lead to a breakthrough."

Adir whipped out his notebook and excitedly wrote down a note to himself.

Grasp the Contradiction.
Every breakdown will lead
to a breakthrough.

Adir thought for a beat, then reiterated what Brio had pointed out the night before. "I want to *make things* happen. While you . . . you want things to *just happen*. Right?"

Elgo nodded his head and Adir continued on, "You want to feel. I want to do." Elgo affirmed by grunting.

"I want to explore; you want to stay put. You want to be safe; I don't mind risks." Elgo nodded again. "You want to simplify; I want to grow. And just like in the Mudflats, you tend to want to go back while I want to push forward. Would you say that sums it up?"

Elgo nodded again.

"Are we missing anything?" Conversations with Elgo had to be very straightforward, since the elephant couldn't speak. Yes or no? This way or that way? Like it or hate it?

"Well, geez. That was easy. Brio made 'Grasp the Contradiction' sound like it was a tough deal. We can knock this out in half the time Brio thinks we will. I think I nailed it. Well, *we* nailed it."

Much like the difference of only being *heard* versus being *listened to*, Elgo seemed poised to have Adir dive deeper into more than *what* the contradictions they had were and explore more about *how* they could grasp an awareness of their contradictions. Instead, Adir checked the box and looked back at the Solution Loop dangling from a hair on Elgo's head. He knew the next clue would be Seek Alignment.

"But where to next?" he said, leaving Elgo wanting more.

Adir looked right. Elgo slowly looked left. Adir looked left as Elgo responded by looking right. There were no visual clues.

As was his tendency, Adir sat down to think. He took a twig that had been scrubbed from a baobab tree they passed on entering the forest. Adir twisted it, then placed it into his mouth. Staring up, ribbons of light, sent by the sun, danced through the baobab canopy.

They both heard a sound. "*Who? Who? Who?*"

It was too high pitched to be Brio, but it had to be an owl, just a smaller one.

"*Who? Who? Who?*" rang out again.

"Elgo, if I was a betting ant, which I am, I'd say Seek Alignment has to do with 'who.' Who seeks the alignment? Let's see if that's our clue."

Elgo didn't move as he still wanted more from Adir. Had the ant explored this hesitation, he would have uncovered more about their contradictory traits. But Adir was caught up in the game and not the lesson at hand.

"Elgo," said Adir, "let's get aligned here. We have a clue, and I say it's worth checking out. How about you?"

The elephant, used to being ushered into yet another idea by his enthusiastic ant, shrugged and gathered up his significant mass to head in the direction of the hooting owl.

"*Who? Who? Who?*" they heard in the distance.

Within ten minutes, Elgo spotted two grass owls facing off. "*Who?*" would cry one, while jutting its feathery head toward the other.

"*Who?*" A head would go back.

"*Who?*" said the other, poking its head forward, then back.

"*Who?*"

As Elgo approached, the two owls turned, wide eyed and jaws dropped, before flying off in opposite directions. Elgo didn't even watch them; his attention was locked on something else.

Adir tried to see what Elgo saw. It was not until they were a few feet from a pair of baobab trees that leaned away from each other that Adir was able to see the note placed at elephant eye level on a branch that extended between the two trees. "Clever," he thought to himself.

Adir walked out along the crest of Elgo's brow to retrieve the next phase. To the right of the plumeria Solution Loop, Adir threaded elephant hair through the hole at the top of the Grasp the Contradiction message from Brio. Then he said, "Let's see," as he licked his finger and eased the first page open. "The Second Phase is Seek Alignment. It's important that you let go of any fixation on 'being right.' Commit to collaborate. Don't dictate. Don't manipulate. Spend the time necessary to be 100 percent aligned. No shortcuts, and you will learn why."

Adir grabbed his notebook and expanded on the concept of Seek Alignment.

Seek Alignment:
Let go of "being right."
Commit to collaborate.

Adir put his notebook to the side, sat back, still with the twig in his mouth, and assumed his thinking position. "Elgo, we agreed on collaborating. Didn't we? I mean, I take my ideas, mesh them with your ideas. Boom. We collaborate by grasping the contradiction." Elgo was unresponsive.

Adir had forgotten about his blind-spot bias. When Adir thought he was aligning, he was more in the mode of thinking he had to convince Elgo of his point of view. The elephant knew when he was being manipulated. Having the ant attempt to convince Elgo of anything was not in the spirit of collaboration or alignment. But Elgo had no words. Only feelings. And his feeling was misalignment.

Adir could tell his buddy was not comfortable. Without taking the time to uncover the truth, the ant switched into solution mode.

"I get it. You're unsure about this forest. You don't like uncertainty," said Adir with confidence. Elgo was rigid and at odds with Adir's take on the situation.

Adir glanced over at the plumeria petals. "Elgo, we are fighters. Right? We don't give up. You proved it in the Mudflats. You didn't give up. You just fought through it until we got to the other side."

Elgo twisted his head. It wasn't a *no*. It wasn't a *yes*. Adir was imposing his bias for drive and determination as an all-important trait to fight through the challenge. In fact, what he dismissed was the motivating pull Elgo felt for reuniting with their colony. Elgo could feel this treasure hunt going awkwardly sideways. It wasn't a game. It was a one-way exercise in what Adir wanted to do.

Faced with this frustration, Elgo retreated his emotions in the direction of security and safety. Adir picked up on this familiar reaction by his elephant.

"Elgo, I know you want to be safe, but don't forget those frustrating months after the earthquake. We got past frustration by working together. I'm with you to make it happen for us."

Elgo was reflexively disillusioned with Adir's focus. This had happened before. Adir was not focused on any alignment. There was no two-way collaboration. Adir focused on convincing his elephant to change his mind to an ant's point of view. The "who, who, who" owls had Adir assuming they were hooting about him. His focus was inward and not on his elephant. The one-way conversation only got worse.

"Let's do this alignment thing, Elgo!" said Adir, giving Elgo hope. "We both push through. Just like the fighters we are, we push on." Adir didn't wait for a response, nor did he notice Elgo's shoulders fold down. "I have to say, we're strong, too. Look at you. You're all muscle and sinew. If it's not happening, you and I both put our heads down and use our willpower and force our way through. That's how we got this far!"

Elgo groaned in resistance.

"Listen, my friend, I know you want to go back," surmised Adir.

Elgo groaned again.

"C'mon, Elgo. We can do this together."

Adir jumped up. While he heard another sound, he had all but turned off his antennae to the state of futility that Elgo felt about his relationship with Adir.

It was a lilting, high-pitched, ascending sound. Some sort of cockatoo that sounded like it was saying *"Whyyy? Whyyy? Whyyy?"* always scooping up to a high note.

"Are they saying 'Why?' The two owls over there were 'whoing' about us. Brio said it himself: 'No shortcuts, and you will know why.' He set up these next creatures to say 'Whyyyy? Whyyy? Whyyy?'" said Adir, mimicking the upward lilt in the next clue of where to go.

Elgo went from rigid to frosty. He sat on his haunches and folded his front two legs across his chest.

Exasperated, Adir pointed at the Solution Loop plumeria. "Sitting here won't get us there," said the ant, now pointing in the direction of the incessant *"Whyyy? Whyyy? Whyyy?"*

Adir continued, "Elgo? You, are you curious? After all, curiosity is the next phase. Curiosity! Curiosity, Elgo. Curiosity."

Elgo slowly looked over in the direction of the sound. Although it was an unconscious habit for the ant and the elephant, and they had never taken the time to truly comprehend the nature of their collective dysfunction, it was a familiar pattern. First, Adir would insist until he got his way. Next, Elgo would succumb to the pressure and acquiesce. Then, disillusioned, Elgo would go along, while Adir, the balance of the time, thought they were aligned.

Elgo rolled forward onto all fours and ambled in the direction of the *"Whyyy? Whyyy? Whyyy?"* Adir, ignorant of his lack of grasping the contradiction and complete misread on alignment, was excited about finding the next clue.

This tree was easy to find. At the very top, the trunk split into two distinct and equal canopies. It made for an artistic "Y." Again at eye level, the note was simple to retrieve. Adir quickly flipped over "the Third Phase" parchment to reveal a longer message from Brio.

Adir cleared his throat and spoke clearly to Elgo, while the elephant was barely listening. "The third step is Stay Curious. This step may take time. Maintain your alignment despite your contradictory perspectives. You may tend to believe your way is the right way. Answer this question to yourself: 'Did I let go of my way being the right way?'

"Adir, this would be like you are both in the same vehicle. But it has two steering wheels. You are determined to steer the vehicle with your wheel. Meanwhile, Elgo is just as resolute to navigate your transportation with his steering wheel. Now imagine there is a barrier between both of you. Neither of you knows the other is trying to take control. All you know is there is chaos, and your efforts are unsatisfied. You end up somewhere and nowhere all at once. Any attempt at staying curious is impractical if you have not first grasped this contradiction and then let go in order to be aligned with a common steering mechanism.

"Any attempt to Stay Curious is going to frustrate you more, increase the level of confusion, and amplify the chaos if you do not collaborate on a completely different approach to your possible destination.

"At this point, you may fully engage in unlimited possibility. Stay in curiosity for as long as it takes to answer these questions:

- "What is it about the other that makes them think, act, and believe?
- "How does that compare to how I think, act, and believe?
- "What am I thinking that I could let go of?
- "What actions are not serving me anymore?
- "What beliefs do I have that work against any chance of collaboration?

"If there is any hint of 'My way is the right way,' or 'You just need to let go of that steering wheel because I've got this,' then you will be alone in your thinking. The second you tug on the wheel with your 'right' idea, you will get an opposing tug on the wheel and be left with confusion. On the other hand, by letting go and committing to a yet-to-be-revealed option of getting to that solution you seek, you and your partner will find yourselves driving in aligned unison. Take time and communicate your differences in the way you think, act, and believe to know *what* needs your attention."

Adir paused for a moment and thought out loud, "Curious? We're always curious." He didn't feel any need to communicate with Elgo because he knew they would be curious about the next step. Elgo was intent on having Adir talk this step through, but his ant partner whipped out his notebook and started writing.

Stay Curious.
What is it about the other that makes them think, act, and believe?

Adir placed the "Seek Alignment" note to the right of "Grasp the Contradiction." He placed "Stay Curious" beside it while Elgo loped aimlessly back into the next clearing. Adir admired how the clues for the Solution Loop were neatly in a row. "We're halfway there, Elgo."

At that very instant, they heard a sound, even farther into the welcoming forest. From down a slight hill came the groan of a bullfrog in guttural, low tones, slowly croaking, *"Whaaat? Whaaat? Whaaat?"*

Adir snapped his head around. He pointed excitedly and said, "That way, Elgo. That way!" As Elgo walked mechanically in the direction of the bullfrog's low and slow beckoning call, Adir continued with his interpretation of the game. "The 'Who?' was about us. The 'Why?' was obviously about our curiosity. The 'What?' has everything to do with what level of creativity we can bring to the Solution Loop."

Elgo didn't respond. He had resigned to walking and no more. As Elgo reached a decline in the forest floor, they saw a spring-fed pond in the quaint basin of low grass and ferns. The bullfrog was sitting on a massive, one-foot lily pad. Beside it was another lily pad with a note on it. "How does Brio get these creatures to play along?" he said to Elgo, whose focus had changed from following the sound to getting a drink of water. Adir was locked in on the clue waiting for them to retrieve it. As Elgo extended his trunk into the water, Adir assumed his elephant was reaching for the next phase in the Solution Loop.

"What the?" said Adir. "The note. Get the note. Let's get me the clue and you can drink later."

Elgo paused, continued to curl his trunk to his mouth, drink, then extended and maneuvered the end of his trunk to pick up the note. He delivered it up over his head and in front of Adir.

"Thanks, buddy. Okay, ready?" said Adir as he opened the message to the first page and read out loud while Elgo continued the routine of drawing water into his trunk and squirting the cool, fresh liquid into his mouth.

"Your next phase is a natural extension of staying curious. Be Creative is about narrowing your focus from unlimited opportunity to a few creative options. If you bring back the vehicle metaphor, this would be a creative mechanism, like a single steering wheel with a handle on each side for you both to operate in tandem. Or you could have a tiller-type stick to lever right or left turns. You would both operate the tiller while constantly communicating your intentions. Or maybe there's another solution you come up with. The point of Be Creative is that you communicate and narrow down your options to the best possible ideas. Take as much time as you need to Be Creative with this scenario.

"Imagine you have reached the edge of the Maswali Forest and you have a number of paths to choose from. Each one has merit. You would communicate a possible solution by reminding yourselves that you want to reconnect with your colony. One path clearly points directly toward the northeast but another path takes you toward the river that ends up in the same place. You creatively devise an idea that a raft on the river will be faster, with less effort, and cover more ground."

Elgo burped.

"Nice," said Adir as he reached for his notepad.

Be Creative.
Narrow your focus from
unlimited opportunity
to a few creative options.

As Adir put a period at the end of his note, a sound seeped through the foliage directly to their right. "Could this sound be the next clue?" thought Adir.

It was not a forest animal this time. It had a more haunting, lingering, sonorous tone. It came from the southern perimeter of the Maswali trees.

The closer they approached, the more it sounded like air being pushed past the hole of a massive jug. They were compelled to follow the hollow note—Adir knew it was a clue. Maybe it was a bird, after all. Brio, maybe? Probably it was him placing the next clue on a baobab tree.

The closer they approached the strange sound, the nearer they trekked to the perimeter, the more they felt rolling waves of heat. At one point, they thought they heard the flap of large wings, and then they found the next note lying on the ground. It looked distressed, as if Brio had hastily thrown it down on the path. "There it is, Elgo, the fifth clue in the treasure hunt!"

Elgo pinched it with the end of his trunk and lifted it up and back over his head.

Excited, anticipating the next message, Adir grabbed it and loudly read Brio's careful handwriting.

"The Fifth Phase is Identify a Solution. The creativity you apply to a variety of options eventually collapses into one action that works for both of you. Establish common ground on which you and your partner can attempt to get traction. You, Adir, have your reality (doing, exploring, risking, growing). Elgo has his reality (feeling, resting, safety, simplifying). Together, you will find your way. Like which path in front of you will work best. You must agree on it and put everything you have into this one possible solution. This played out in your journey when you were stymied in the Mudflats. Yet, when you refocused on your colony and getting back to your family, you 100 percent committed yourselves into action. You marched straight ahead . . ."

That was the end of the message. Adir flipped it over, but the other side of the paper was blank. He turned the paper back to the message and repeated the last four words: "You marched straight ahead . . ."

Adir was thrilled. The game of the treasure hunt had given them a formula that would reunite them with their colony and offer them an escape from the stuckness. So he whipped out his notebook and wrote down the next part of the Solution Loop.

Identify a **Solution**.

Collapse all options into

one action that works

for both of you.

Adir hung the tattered note beside all the others. Grasp the Contradiction, followed by Seek Alignment, Stay Curious, Be Creative, and Identify a Solution. He glanced at the Solution Loop plumeria and verbally announced the final petal to Elgo. "Take Action."

Adir scoured their surroundings, then spotted some sort of letter in the sand. From a distance, it looked like an "A" for Action. Upon a closer look, it was obviously a huge arrow scratched into the desert floor. Two sentinel baobab trees towered overhead, each leaning slightly toward their twin, as if forming a gateway to their future. The lancet arch framed the arrow, pointing south into the enormous Potea Desert. Warm air blew through the gateway. This was also the source of the sound they heard.

Elgo gulped, and Adir sensed his elephant's discomfort.

"Elgo, Brio's sent us a sign. He must have skipped the note and inscribed an arrow as the simplest clue of all. Take Action!

"This is our path, buddy. We GOT this. We must Stay Curious and go straight. We got through the Mudflats. We can get through this." Adir's voice trailed off as he took in the expanse in front of them.

"This has to be it, Elgo. C'mon. Let's do this."

Elgo did not move. What he saw in front of him was more struggle and uncertainty. Then Adir, remembering what had worked in the Mudflats, said words that reinspired Elgo. "Let's do this for our colony. Our family is waiting for us and it will take both of us to get there. Let's Take Action."

Ignited by the faint hope of a reunion with their family on the other side of the desert, and also knowing that Adir wouldn't stop insisting, Elgo took measured steps onto the hot sand floor.

"Yea baby!" squealed Adir as they set foot onto the hot surface. "South. WE. GO!" Adir grabbed his notebook. He completed all his notes and ended with two words: "Take Action."

Meanwhile, high atop the sentinel gateway, Valafar and his vulture cohort watched the gullible ant and elephant plod toward certain death. Valafar grabbed a crumpled parchment of baobab leaves from his companion. He flipped the Sixth Phase over and read handwriting by the one animal he despised above all others: Brio the Owl.

In his gravelly voice, he croaked with amusement, "The Sixth Phase is Take Action. This is where you put your best-guess solution into action. Your focused activity in rebuilding your home in the Oasis didn't work. Action without going through all the phases in the Solution Loop is equivalent to a waste of time and effort. While you attempted a new life in the Vine Spot, you learned a little about the contradiction between what motivated you and what inspired Elgo. When you learned to let go of that metaphorical steering wheel of being right, you will find there were unlimited possibilities as part of curiosity. When you and Elgo narrow down those possibilities, you can be more creative with your options. From there, you Identify a Solution that is worth chasing. If that solution doesn't work and it has no traction, then you cycle back into the loop again as you start at Grasping the Contradiction. On the flip side, if the possible solution you put into action has traction, you have found your way out of stuckness.

"Now, turn north through the forest. You'll find me on the banks of Black Rock River. I have a raft with your name on it. As we float down the river toward your colony, we can chat about all you learned about each other on your own special treasure hunt."

Valafar paused, looked at the tracks Elgo left on the sandy ground. "Solution? If a death march is a solution for us to pick the meat off their dead bones, then that sounds like a good solution to me!"

Also written on the note that Valafar had ensured the ant and the elephant had no chance to read was:

Take Action.

Action with traction exits the cycle.

Still stuck? Go through

the cycle again.

The vultures looked at each other.

"Two days?" said one.

"Four," responded Valafar. "Then we follow the sweet smell of death wafting up into the clouds."

Valafar glanced at the note in his left claw before crumpling it viciously and tossing it forward.

It tumbled down onto the middle of the arrow that pointed to Adir and Elgo's doom.

ADIR'S NOTES TO SELF

- Grasp the Contradiction: Every breakdown will lead to a breakthrough.
- Seek Alignment: Let go of "being right." Commit to collaborate. Don't dictate. Don't manipulate. Spend the time necessary to be 100 percent aligned.
- Stay Curious: What does my companion think, act, and believe? And why?
- Be Creative: Narrow my focus from unlimited opportunity to a few creative options.
- Identify a Solution: Collapse all options into one actionable idea that works for both of us.

CHAPTER 8

Adapt or Die

After hours in the desert, Adir started to question the rationale of their decision—or, if he were being honest, *his* decision—to go marching off into this hot expanse of sand.

The landscape stretched in disorienting sameness in every direction. For a while, they'd tried to use the tall baobabs as a reference point, but by afternoon, the trees were no longer in sight. They had to rely solely on the location of the sun.

They had brought no stores of food or water, were traveling south when their colony was headed northeast. They had no clue when they would know where to turn and meet back up with their colony. The situation was not ideal.

That evening, with no end in sight, Adir and Elgo camped at the top of a sand dune.

The moon hadn't yet lifted past the horizon, but billions of stars already lit the sky. Adir looked up and easily spotted the Southern Cross. Its location never changed; it rotated on itself every twenty-four hours. If they continued to head directly south, in the direction of the Southern Cross, they would end up where Brio intended for them to go. Adir felt reassured: they would be able to orient themselves no matter what time of day.

The next morning, they woke up as the cool desert of the night gave way to the sun-blistered desert of the day. Adir locked in on the direction he'd noted just prior to sleeping the night before, angling them that way.

They were nauseously thirsty and hungry. Elgo groaned for all those reasons and more, his negative thoughts surging in waves of increasing intensity.

"Come on, Elgo, we are in the sweet spot of activity," encouraged Adir, belying his doubts. "We would not be on this path if Brio didn't know of a worthy destination. I bet there are juicy kiwifruits waiting for us. Big bowls of heavy red apples. Stacks of bananas and, most of all, cool, fresh well water. We will drink until it sloshes around our tummies like . . . like . . . like water sloshing around in our bellies."

Elgo brought himself to his feet, but was confused about which way to go.

Confidently, Adir proclaimed, "That way, my friend. It's exactly that way."

So they walked.

The heat was bad in the morning, but intensified to brutal by midday. No water. No shade. No food. Their pace slowed.

It didn't help when they saw a large inverted skeleton of a water buffalo partly submerged from months of desert storms. The two horns and skull were a couple of feet from the upturned rib cage. They pretended not to let it bother them as they walked right by.

Adir didn't want to scare Elgo, but he could sense his elephant's desperation. By late afternoon, Adir spotted a line in the sand. It appeared like a creek or a stream. Waves of heat distorted everything at eye level. Dunes expanded and compressed as surges of heat mixed with the air and blurred reality in its wake. The fuzzy optics of a mirage were in every distant direction. The only thing crystal clear was the immediate edges of dunes to their right or left contrasted with the deep blue of the sky.

Adir ran to the front edge of Elgo's brow. "Elgo. There! See that?" Elgo, unsure what Adir was talking about, peripherally followed the pointed finger.

Then, hope turned into disappointment. The undulating line he saw was not a creek but someone else's tracks.

They scoured the landscape for clues. Who were these others? Where were they going? Did they know a better way? The path aligned approximately with Adir and Elgo's direction, so they decided to follow it to the highest dune a quarter mile away to what they thought was the southwest.

But at the top, their optimism turned to anguish. The trail they had followed led directly to a pile of bones. A skeleton . . . a water buffalo's remains.

These were Adir and Elgo's tracks. They had spent the entire day trudging in a circle.

A switch went off in Elgo's head. He sat down and simply gave up. No sound. No groans. No spirit. Elgo leaned over and lay on his side.

It took Adir an hour to convince Elgo to rest in the shade of the sand dune. By early evening, Elgo's breathing started to come back to normal. Each breath was punctuated with an unsettling sound of dry leaves being ground along a rough rock.

Adir's mind was racing. He glanced over at the direction Brio had pointed out for them. *A breakdown would lead to a breakthrough.*

Adir thought to himself, "No food or water seems like a total breakdown! Like we're going to die here. What breakthrough could there possibly be?"

Adir turned that thought over in his mind. "What breakthrough?" he repeated out loud. Contradiction is an entirely normal part of a relationship between entities. "I wonder if there is more to this contradiction than just our relationship?" mumbled Adir. "What other relationships are we dealing with?"

The ant was silent for a few minutes, then two words popped into his mind. Mother Nature.

"Maybe we need to look at the relationship between nature and us?"

Adir staved off desperation and decided to go through each step of the Solution Loop. He thought out loud because he knew Elgo was listening.

"What relationship exists between nature and us? Well, I don't particularly like rules. I like to ignore anyone who says I can't do something. Mother Nature has rules and she won't bend them. If we try to break them, we suffer the consequences. Hence, a contradiction in mannerisms we should grasp. So, given this desperate situation, we need to find a way to align with Mother Nature herself since she's not going to align with us."

Elgo roused with a semblance of curiosity.

"How to align? Immediately start getting curious. But about what? What makes me tick when times get tough? I set out to compete. I aim to win. I want to succeed. What drives you, Elgo? You like security and staying safe. I'm quite sure I haven't helped you feel comfortable at all.

"I definitely did not help things after the earthquake. I couldn't stop thinking, 'Why is this happening? What am I missing? Have I lost my ability to win?' That had to have impacted you. Now, here we are, and couple my old thoughts with Mother Nature's rule that if we don't get food or water in this desert, we'll die and—"

Elgo let out a small groan.

"We're not going to die, Elgo. Let's Be Creative. We're experiencing a setback, but we need to fight for what we want." Echoes of a conversation they'd had with Brio right after the earthquake resurfaced.

"Remember what Brio said last year? *When disaster strikes, we do the opposite of what we need to do. When we're falling, we fight it.* Elgo, remember the time we fell down the huge hill near our destroyed home? I hurt my arms and ankle. All this because I fought the entire way down the fall. Remember how you were unscathed?

"Mother Nature has this little thing called gravity. Fight it and you lose. Go with it and you have a shot at winning. The solution we need here is to *Go with it*. There's no water. No food. So let's Take Action and go where Mother Nature has water and food.

"Elgo, I made a mistake. I let my ego get in the way. What felt like me trying to problem-solve was really a case of me, again, determined to be right. I made being right more important than staying alive. I remember Brio saying once, 'Ego means carrying pain and suffering like bearing two pails of rocks on both shoulders.' I've just realized that my ego is a burden not worth carrying anymore."

Ego means carrying pain
and suffering
like bearing two pails of
rocks on both shoulders.

Adir added, "Having to be right makes alignment impossible. When I was younger, my parents were 'the Law.' They told me the way things were going to be, and that was that. But I would dig in and refuse to cede any ground. It was a power struggle. A standoff.

"Then, I'd be punished. It makes sense. They were the adults, trying to teach me about right from wrong and consequences, and I was busy trying to prove them wrong. There was no way for us to find common ground, much like the Potea Desert has no intention of finding common ground with me and you. How can a solution stand a chance in a dynamic where one side is intractable and the other side is resigned?"

He continued, giving voice to his thoughts. "When the other side is nonnegotiable, like Mother Nature right now, then we need to"—he paused again, then spoke one word that had an immediate effect on Elgo—"adapt. Adapt! Remember our horrible day in the Splitnit rapids? We learned quickly that our survival relied on our ability to adapt. We adapt or we die."

Adir went on. "Remember, Elgo? There was no forcing our way with a river flow that was unrelenting. When we fought against the current, we were in danger of drowning, being pummeled, or getting caught. When we went with the flow, we eventually found a way out. When it rains, we blend with the oncoming force and find shelter until it passes. Here we are in the most inhospitable, uncompromising place possible and we are trying to negotiate our path. As if we learned nothing from the rapids! If we go on like this, of course there is no way we will find a solution.

"When the other side is immovable, we need to adapt, blend, find a mindset that will be the way out of being stuck in dysfunction. Buddy, we've got to go back. I know you want to rest, but Mother Nature's rules don't bend. If we don't go back, without water, in this heat, we will be vulture food. Plus, we circled back. We are a full night's walk back to the forest."

Elgo was scared and uncertain.

"The moonlight and the Southern Cross will guide us. If we keep directly south behind us, we will surely find our way back to the Maswali Forest, which is fully stocked with water and food. This is a fight we can win by blending with nature, embracing what she has to offer, not pushing back. It's cool at night—that's the perfect time to travel without further dehydrating ourselves. When we get to the forest, we will have all the water we want. I bet there is a banana tree that has a sign: 'Elgo's Banana Emporium.'"

Elgo allowed a slight grin.

It was time to turn back.

The night walk was arduous but somehow magical. Part of that magic stemmed from how ecstatic Elgo was to go back to the safety of the Maswali Forest. He was physically tired but buoyed to the action of letting go of dead ends.

The other part of the magic came from the landscape of the desert at night. It was soothing and awe-inspiring. There was beauty in its nothingness and infinite potential.

Adir looked at the Solution Loop plumeria. Stars sparkled their reflection off the medallion's shiny surface.

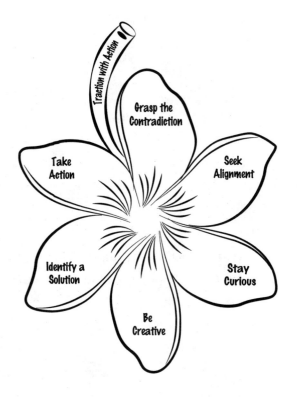

On their return trek to the forest, Adir grappled with the fact that this had clearly not been a solution. They needed to do something else to become more aligned.

Deep into the night, a few hours before sunrise, they spotted the dark tips of the baobab canopies. Something was flying toward them. Within seconds, it was possible to make out their nocturnal friend, Brio, coming at them at an alarming speed.

"Stop. Stop. Stop!" he said breathlessly as he landed on Elgo's back.

"Brio, we're so sorry we didn't stay on our journey into the desert like you instructed. But we just—"

Brio interrupted their apology. "Wait, I never instructed you to do that."

"Yes, you did. You scratched an arrow in the sand under the leaning baobab trees."

"I did see that but didn't scratch an arrow. Someone or something clawed that into the sand—and there is only one thing that feeds on dead animals in the desert . . ."

"Vultures," they said in unison.

"Listen," Brio said quietly. "Valafar, the lead vulture, has gone back to get Chromia. The Alpha Wolf has gone insane with anger. Valafar plans to lead Chromia and her pack out tomorrow night to find you both, and kill you."

"What's your plan?" asked Adir.

"It's dangerous, but I think it can work. We need to backtrack, retracing your *exact footsteps*. Elgo, can you do that the rest of the way?"

Elgo nodded.

"Good. Then we quickly drink and eat while we backtrack until we can disguise our tracks by entering the bullfrog pond and carefully traveling upstream to the northern exit of the Maswali Forest. About this time, by my calculations, Chromia and her pack will be blind with fury, following your scent *into* the forest and out into the desert.

"Our lives depend on how fast we get back up the trail and lose our scent, evading overhead exposure to Valafar and his gang."

"Run?" gasped Adir.

"We have no choice. This is life and death," replied Brio.

"Once we hit the open plains north of the Maswali Forest, how do we lose our scent there?"

"White Rock Creek. But that's ten miles from the northern trailhead."

"That is a lot of running."

"I know, but that's our only option. If we get to the creek, the water flow will mask our scent the same way it did at Mill Creek. Then we're safe to move back east and find the colony."

Brio paused, looked at his friends, and said, "What do you think?"

Adir looked around at the desert and back at Brio. "Sounds a whole lot better than dying of a combination of dehydration, hunger, exhaustion, and being torn limb from limb by a pack of wolves while vultures watch, waiting for their chance to pick at our remains."

"Ewwwww," said Brio.

Elgo shuddered.

ADIR'S NOTES TO SELF

- Ego carries pain and suffering like bearing two pails of rocks on both shoulders.
- Keep revisiting the Solution Loop until we get traction.
- When faced with an outside force that is nonnegotiable . . . Adapt.
- My curiosity almost killed us. I broke the rule of not letting go of the steering wheel.

CHAPTER 9

Death's Back Door

As the group cautiously moved from point to point in the Maswali Forest, Elgo regained his strength with every step. Adir took a few moments to jot down lessons from their near-death experience in the desert. Brio took the opportunity to quiz them on their progress with the Solution Loop.

"I learned a massive lesson, Brio," said Adir. "The Solution Loop goes to hell when Taking Action is no longer a direction but a fight to survive. Once we aligned with finding food and water, we curiously looked at all our options. Creatively decided to travel at night with the help of stars to guide us and the cool night. Then—"

"Shhhhhhhh," hissed Elgo, making the most noise he could.

Off in the distance, ahead of them, they heard the unmistakable sound of a pack of wolves beating on the trail.

Elgo barely had time to roll and pin himself up behind the nearest baobab.

One second Brio and Adir were talking about the Solution Loop on Elgo's back. The next second, they were on the forest floor, frozen in disbelief that twenty thousand pounds could move that quickly.

A heartbeat later, they dropped in the deep grass. Within a few seconds, dozens of wolf paws thrashed at the trail around them. Only luck and the tall grass saved them from detection.

As the sound faded into the belly of the forest, Brio yelled in a whisper, "RUN!!!"

Elgo deftly bounded over to Adir and Brio. In one scoop of his trunk, he gathered them up and ran down the hill, into the pond, and up the spring-fed creek. After a mile of stumbling on unstable and slippery river rock, they reached the northern trailhead.

"Okay, guys, the second we step out of the creek and onto the trail, Elgo needs to run. Load up on water because it will be hot and dry under the harsh sun."

After a minute of drinking and eating a few bananas that were hanging over the creek, Brio asked as quietly as he could, "Ready?"

Elgo nodded as Adir ensured his notepad was safe and he had a good hold of a stout elephant hair. "Go!" said Brio.

Elgo's gait resembled a stubby-legged horse, running at a full gallop. Their trail would be easy for the wolves to track, but, since the pack would not find out they were not in the desert until well into the night, they should have a head start. So Elgo didn't worry about covering his tracks and just focused on getting them to the next creek as quickly as possible.

With every mile, panic slid more toward relief, but after five miles, Elgo couldn't maintain his super-elephant pace. Both Brio and Adir assured him that it was all right to slow down.

"Son, you need to pace yourself. You'll bonk and you're done for."

"Bonk?" asked Adir.

"The wall. The point where your body has nothing left when brought to the limit of exhaustion. An antelope friend of mine named Galloway . . . Listen, never mind. We are halfway to the White Rock Creek crossing. We must stay focused. How are you doing, Elgo?"

Elgo shook his head and picked his loping back up into a steady gallop. His physical stamina was impressive.

"Oh no!" cried Adir, looking and pointing up.

The collaboration between the vultures and wolves resulted in a shared tactic: the wolves' habit of having a wolf sweep at the back of the pack was being employed by the gang of vultures. In this case, the sweep of vultures covered an ellipsis of terrain. One vulture scanned south while a second scanned north.

As Adir and his team looked up, the vulture looked down and recognized them, changing his lazy, gliding pace into a full-speed flight directly south. It headed straight to the teams waiting for nightfall at the edge of the Potea Desert to tell them that there was no need to enter the desert.

Elgo picked up his pace. With one mile to go, Elgo stumbled, falling onto his two front knees. He was sleep deprived and physically exhausted, plus it was too dark to see undulations and turns in the trail.

"C'mon, buddy. Just walk. We've made good time. Keep moving. It starts going downhill in just a few hundred feet," said Brio and Adir, trying desperately to keep Elgo's spirits up.

White Rock Creek was just around the next corner.

But only three quarters of a mile at the trail's bend, the wolves crested the edge of the eastern hill, silhouetted against the full moon rising behind them. Chromia howled in sinister delight.

Elgo lurched forward and stumbled over a fallen log. His momentum plus the steep slope meant he careened toward the wall of trees at the bend in the trail. Luckily, he went with his instincts and allowed the fall to happen rather than fight it.

Brio flew into the air when Elgo started to tumble, but Adir was whipped through the air. He bounded down the hill like an acorn being dropped by a squirrel from an oak tree. At the very last millisecond, Adir reached out and grabbed Elgo's tail. Though it almost ripped Adir's front leg off, he did not let go. Brio looked back as the wolves shook off their surprise at watching Elgo and

Adir fall and bolted down the slope with menacing speed. From the wolves' viewpoint, the elephant disappeared over a roller in the terrain as he directly plummeted toward the creek below. They could tell he hit bottom when treetops shuddered from elephant impact at their base.

"Listen," said Brio to the two dazed friends. "The pack will be expecting you to go downstream or down the trail toward the east. They will assume you want to go in the direction of your colony. Go upstream now! Run as fast as you can, count to ten, stop, hide, and hold still. After they are gone, climb all the way to Saddle Ridge. White Rock Creek splits there. You will have a safe passage on the other side of the saddle. Stay in the stream. I'll catch up to you there. Now, go!"

In the next breath, Brio flew a hundred feet along the creek below. He was screaming at the nonexistent Elgo and Adir downstream in an attempt to throw the wolves off the scent.

Ten. With his trunk, Elgo grabbed Adir and bounded up the stream.

Nine. Round river rocks were hurdles in their ascent.

Eight. They gained distance.

Seven. Farther from the creek, now.

Six. The distant sound of Brio screeching for his friends to escape reached them as he led the wolves away.

Five. *"Run as fast as you can, the wolves are coming,"* Brio yelled, wanting the real Adir and Elgo to hear him, too.

Four. Elgo pulled on a branch overhead.

Three. He sprang from rock, to rock, to rock.

Two. They could barely hear Brio anymore.

One.

They stopped.

Slow breaths.

Deep, slow breaths.

They held still as death.

As the team froze, the wolves rounded the corner and reached the creek crossing. In another heartbeat, they turned downstream toward Brio's rattled shrieks. As the moonlight washed the scene, as if in slow motion, Chromia leaped an impossible twelve feet into the air. The gash across her body and face flashed in the steely moonlight.

Brio thought he was beyond her reach, but she contorted and snatched him from midair. His staged shrieks turned into true, pain-filled, terrified screams. Chromia mercilessly closed her powerful jaws.

Brio went silent and limp as sharp fangs tore into the defenseless owl's neck.

As she landed, she whipped her head from side to side. Brio's entire body cracked, shattering like dry twigs. With a pronounced snap of her head, Chromia's grip broke Brio's neck.

Horrified, still up the hill in hiding, Adir and Elgo watched as their murdered friend was flung up high, thrown over a branch. He was draped over it, limply swaying on an embankment branch.

"That owl carcass is *only* to be eaten by Valafar. He has a score to settle with that owl."

For a couple of seconds, the only sound was that of the babbling brook. The forest was quiet except for water talking its way over thousands of smooth river stones.

Brio's decimated bones, wings, and neck lay on an outstretched tree limb. His once proud frame was lifeless and still.

As the pack careened downstream, more determined than ever, Adir and Elgo knew their only chance to avoid meeting Brio's fate was to retreat over Saddle Ridge. They trudged uphill, numb and broken.

Brio is dead. Brio is dead. Brio is dead.

In **absolute grief** and loss,
there are **no words**
to take away the **pain**, but still,
we must **go forward**.

ADIR'S NOTES TO SELF

- In absolute grief and loss, there are no words to take away the pain.
- Forward we must go.

CHAPTER 10

Rest, Pace, Go with It

They had no words.

They felt just as dead inside as Brio truly was.

Their legs moved but their minds were mired in deep, dark voids.

Their hearts were completely shattered.

As Brio had instructed, Adir and Elgo journeyed over Saddle Ridge and followed the split in White Rock Creek toward Black Rock River. They walked for three days, never exchanging a word. In the daytime, moving masked the pain, but staying still yanked their souls from their bodies. Their nights were filled with tears and the quiet sounds of muffled grief. Each passing moment was torture.

At the end of the third day, the weather turned cold and rainy to match their mood. They pinned themselves up against a rock protrusion at a bend in the stream. Huddling together to stay dry and stave off the cruel drop in temperature, with their heads hung low, they barely noticed a train of ants marching straight through their temporary camp.

One by one, as the ants passed the shattered duo, they looked to the right, then brought their gaze back to their destination. Some ants were carrying bits of leaves. Others transported blades of grass. Two walked by with a grasshopper leg each. Each turning, as if on cue, to take in the huddled friends.

Adir did not bother to say hello. His grief was too much for him to entertain any pleasantries. It may have appeared rude, but it was not uncommon for ants of different colonies to keep to themselves.

To their left, on a rock beside the river, a chameleon lounged with his tongue prepared to dart out and snatch a fly hovering above the surface.[*]

"Flies can't be that bright," thought Adir when another fly flitted over at nearly the same spot and was eaten. Then he thought about where they were and the state they were in. He wondered if he and Elgo were flies and life was a chameleon waiting to snatch them out of existence.

---

[*] Did you hear about the chameleon who had trouble changing colors? He had a reptile dysfunction.

Night came and the friends were alone again. The sound of water slowly rounding the riverbend was a lullaby for their first deep sleep in well over a month.

The heartache loosened its grip for the moment. Sleep came in a single wave of compassion.

Elephants have eyelashes. Some elephants have eyelashes so long and voluminous they are like folding fans, powerful enough to keep the most persistent flies at bay with a blink and a swish.

Adir felt it first, then Elgo noticed bursts of air flapping in their direction as they awoke from their semi-comatose state.

"Agggh," yelped Adir when he saw, through blurry eyes, a massive eyeball and more eyelashes than he thought possible on an elephant. "An ELEPHANT?"

A voice from somewhere above the pachyderm's fetching eyelashes broke the silence: "You're not dead?!" The voice was half surprised, half relieved. "I must have had a thousand ants tell me there was a dead ant and elephant at Black Rock Bend."

"Who are you?" croaked Adir, squinting to take in a backlit, blurry elephant and whatever was riding it.

There was a murmur from behind the nearest elephant. Five other elephants surrounded the scraggly pair of travelers. On the top of each elephant's head sat an ant. Both the elephants and the ants were equally curious about this new discovery.

"I'm Aria," said the lead ant from atop her elephant. She was confident and commanded the space. "This here is Ella. Me and Ella . . . well . . . we're pleased to meet you."

Elgo rolled to sit up straight. Adir scrambled to the top of Elgo's head. "Adir. My name's Adir."

Elgo cleared his throat and raised an eyebrow.

"This is Elgo."

"Let's gather your things and head over to our Herd Camp," said Aria.

All the elephants nodded and swayed in a welcoming approval.

Adir made sure they still had his notebook in the fold of Elgo's skin. He looked at where the plumeria should be, but it was lost in their most recent tumble downhill.

"We'll follow you," he said.

Once at camp, there were more elephants in one place than Adir had ever seen in his life. Each one had an ant companion.

But the most interesting thing to Adir was not the number of elephants—it was Aria.

Aria was the kind of ant who knew where she was going in life, with a spunky attitude that was instantly engaging. Her elephant, Ella, had the same kind of persona. Ella would look straight at you with her massive eyelashes and bright, knowing eyes. They were the most self-assured team Adir and Elgo had ever met.

The herd invited Adir and Elgo to join them for a meal and made a space for them to rest if they chose to stay. As they settled in a circle around the food and water, Adir told them about his and Elgo's journey. He explained the earthquake and the personal aftershocks that rocked their lives. He talked in emotional detail about his struggle to rebuild on broken ground in what was left of the Oasis. With each word, he relived the experience in painful detail.

He spoke of his disdain for Chromia and her multiple attempts on his life. How her breath smelled like chewed, raw meat and how she would not stop until he and Elgo were dead. He expounded on the strength and fortitude Elgo had shown in the Mudflats, the Potea Desert, and their narrow escape from the Maswali Forest.

His voice breaking when he got to Brio's death, he described how Brio had sacrificed his life to save them, barely able to get the words out.

A smattering of oxpeckers making an uninvited visit to the backs of surrounding elephants snapped their gaze and took notice of the conversation.

"Where?" asked Aria. "Where did this happen to Brio?"

"Just east of White Rock Creek and the main trail."

A loud snap like the crack of a whip sounded through the gathering as a couple dozen oxpeckers flew off in the general direction of White Rock Creek. After all, Brio was a popular guy. Most creatures with or without wings had known of him, so the news of his passing shocked everyone.

As the oxpeckers flew directly north in the direction of Brio's demise, Adir and Elgo shuddered to imagine what they would find.

An hour of storytelling led Adir to relay Brio's lessons about the Solution Loop. With a stick, he carved a replica of the now lost treasure, the six-petal plumeria flower.

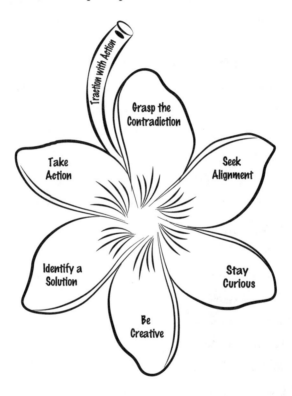

This flower fascinated Aria and Ella. They related to the concept of embracing each other's differences to find alignment. Aria identified with Elgo's tendency toward feeling and being in the moment. She remarked how she and Ella thrived when they had projects that were urgent. She also revealed how her elephant's instant responses were a part of what she called "the joy of spontaneity." "I love trusting Ella's first instinct. It has never steered us wrong," Aria added. This led to the phases in the Solution Loop of Staying Curious with infinite possibilities and Being Creative by narrowing actionable ideas into a possible solution.

"Slowing down at the curious phase makes so much sense. I think we tend to feel what's right and just react. If there are unlimited possibilities, then spending extra time on letting all the ideas bake makes sense," said Aria.

Aria reflected before asking, "Is the 'Be Creative' just as careful of a selection?"

"I heard Brio say once, 'A good idea won't go away,'" said Adir.

A good idea won't go away.

"Do you ever have problems with too many good ideas?" asked Aria.

"All the time," injected Adir on the heels of Aria's question. "But the best ideas for the time surface, even if you have to go through the loop a few times."

Without a formula of phases, like the Solution Loop, Aria felt that she and her elephant had been doing something similar. But her enthusiasm for putting this sequence to the test after future setbacks would lead to breakthroughs in their lives.

As the conversation wound down, and mealtime satiated all and was long past, the herd realized that Adir and Elgo were still beat from their physical and emotional journey, so Aria and Ella showed them to their makeshift bed. Within seconds, both Adir and Elgo were sound asleep, resting not only their bodies, but their hearts as well, feeling lighter because they'd shared their burden through conversation.

Days passed as Adir and Elgo regained their resilience and energy.

As they conversed with Aria and Ella, Adir and Elgo gained perspective on the effects the earthquake had had on them.

Aria said it best one day: "Adir. Elgo. Don't let the earthquake define you. In fact, stop dwelling on your earthquake story! Period. You're allowing the earthquake to stay in your head rent-free. Both of you are holding on to your past with a death grip."

> Stop dwelling on your earthquake story.
> You're allowing it to stay in your head rent-free.

"How do you know this?" asked Adir.

"I know it because I lived it," responded Aria. "I haven't shared this story in years, but allow me to give you an example. When I was a young adult, our family of ants and elephants were attacked by a pride of lions who came all the way down here from the northern Savannah. We were heartbroken by our massive losses—particularly the death of a one-year-old calf.

"But the worst loss we experienced came from aftershocks following the attack. Our '*earthquake*,'" she said with air quotes, "was losing a precious young one, but the emotional aftershocks affected us for months and years afterward. Some of our pack, especially the mother elephant, became depressed to the point of needing constant care. We worried the mother would hurt herself. It was horrible.

"Then, about eighteen months after the assault, three of our pack came down with E. coli and two of our family members had severe heart issues, something that should never happen with elephants in their prime.

"We lost our little one once. But we kept repeating the story of his loss over and over until we learned that personal devastation can infect the thoughts so negatively that it may cause actual physical disease up to three years later. By constantly obsessing over our '*earthquake*'"—again with the air quotes—"we forced ourselves to keep wandering through more *dis-ease* of the mind and body."

"Did everyone keep repeating the story?" asked Adir.

"The story was repeated verbally and experientially," admitted Aria. "It was not until we each made a conscious effort to stop reliving the memory of it that things got better. We took the word 'disease' and modified it in relation to our thoughts and feelings. We now call these notions *dis-ease*, or the opposite of 'ease.' Dis-ease is the precursor to disease. Dis-ease is the antithesis of wellness. Repeating the earthquake story is the definition of dis-ease." Aria looked directly into Adir's eyes as her own watered up. "This is what you are doing to yourselves, Adir."

Aria reached out and put her hand on Adir and he looked up. She continued, "You are reliving the earthquake in the Oasis and reliving what you could have done differently to save Brio. Not only are you ruminating on the past, but you're dwelling on forces beyond your control. There was nothing you could do then, and there's nothing you can do to change it now. The only option you have is to pivot away from the thoughts that are pulling you down. Replace them with thoughts of reuniting with your colony. Imagine being back with your family."

Elgo shuddered with a classic elephant buzz. Adir felt the same way.

"We had a similar experience in the Mudflats. It wasn't until Elgo and I refocused our attention on reuniting with our family that were we able to carry on."

"Exactly," said Aria, nodding. "You have the choice to be tormented with dis-ease, and make yourself sick from past experiences. But you can also choose to pivot to the future that gives you more of those elephant buzzes. Don't allow dis-ease to take hold. The mind and body are connected. After a personal earthquake, emotional, mental, and physical disease must not be allowed to manifest over time."

Don't allow **dis-ease** to take hold.
The mind and body are **connected**.
After a personal earthquake,
emotional, mental, and physical
disease must **not be allowed**.

"We've been avoiding our future because we're afraid of the unknown—like a cactus," said Adir.

"A . . . cactus?" replied Aria.

"During our time in the Vine Spot, Brio taught us to seek the light. To be curious and creative, like a vine. It's time to seek the light and grow some more. If Brio were here, he would have us start by getting a firm grasp on our contradictions. We're better off understanding how differently we each approach challenges and opportunities. We basically seek the light of understanding each other."

"But you've been together day and night. Is there stuff you don't know about each other?" asked Aria, with an idea of what the answer would be.

"One hundred percent! We are constantly learning about each other when we take the time to explore. The more questions we ask, the more light we shed on our differences and contradictions. Brio used the word 'grasp' by design. He didn't want us to simply 'get' an idea of our differing approaches to life; he wanted us to embrace our contradictions, grapple with our polarity, understand how our duality can make us stronger."

Adir turned his attention to his elephant. "Elgo, aren't you curious about how we can work together better? Your physical force and powerful habit-forming skills and my mental potency and determination to win combine to give us strengths that really balance each other. If we combine them, we are invincible. There must be countless creative ways we can use your muscle and my brains to break out of this place we keep getting stuck in!"

Elgo knew he liked the security of staying in one place, but, at the same time, he detested the trapped feeling of being stuck. Memories of the Mudflats returned at the thought of being stuck. He started to feel that despondent, grossly inadequate feeling of not being good enough.

Adir, able to tell that Elgo was taking a depressing turn, interrupted this familiar pattern instead of allowing his elephant to drag him into negativity, too. "Elgo, in the past I might say 'Get a grip.' But I'm learning I haven't taken the time to pay closer attention to how you're feeling. Brio would tell us to pivot from the cactus mindset to the vine mindset. He would say we are more than our past."

"I like where Adir is headed here," interjected Aria, excited to be part of the growth. "It's just like our fixation on losing our young one to the lions. To change our horrible results after the loss, we changed our focus from what's wrong to what's right. We lived by a motto, 'To change your results, change your beliefs.' The conflict WE have each experienced is growth waiting to be revealed," said Aria, looking from Elgo up to Adir.

To change your **results**,
change your beliefs.

"Elgo," said Adir, having his turn in the conversation, "this has to do with me as much as you. If we don't one-eighty off negative, familiar feelings, both of us will stay stuck. We must risk finding a new solution. This is not the Potea Desert in front of us, it's just another chapter of uncertainty."

Elgo stood up straighter than normal. He lifted his gaze and held his head higher.

"My friend," said Adir, putting all six feet on Elgo's neck, "*if* we act, you and I together, we not only interrupt the patterns of anxiety, but we can also break free from the muddy trap of our negative thoughts."

Over the past few days, Elgo could feel himself and Adir getting stronger. From their most recent motivational conversation, Aria the Ant and Ella the Elephant continued to be not-so-subtle cheerleaders. They constantly encouraged their new friends to swivel off what hadn't worked in the past toward the direction of health and vitality.

"Guys, I know you're anxious to get back to your colony, but the journey ahead of you is arduous. You do not want to start from a deficit. Give us three weeks and we'll have you primed for any new adventure that awaits," said Aria over breakfast.

Adir and Elgo agreed to build their strength, both physically and mentally.

They began with fitness because Aria knew that fitness routines would give them a sense of normalcy and some endorphins. So, at first, they worked on a little yoga routine with their new elephant friends.* Physical activity gave them a chance to stimulate their blood flow and aerobic fitness. Whether on walks in the nearby forest or swimming in the nearby pond, exercise was also a chance to socialize and rediscover normalcy.

Aria also knew the merit of eating better foods. She inspired Adir and Elgo to stop munching on sugarcane, and start focusing on finding fresh fruits and vegetables. Their chaotic lives had

---

* Picture ten elephants, on ten massive yoga mats, doing the Warrior Pose, followed by Downward Dog (which looks like elephants just standing there).

wrecked their diets. Together, they spent time learning about balanced meals and how appropriate portions made for more energy and regeneration of their immune system. Better meals meant mental clarity. They found themselves improving their mood, just by making better choices at mealtime.

In addition, they spent time meditating twice per day, for twenty-minute intervals. Aria drew from a course she took called Transantental Medantation. First thing in the morning and just before dinner, Adir and Elgo would sit in a quiet place and close their eyes. They would each silently repeat the mantra "Be."

When a thought would appear, they would each find their equanimity and slip back into repeating the "Be" mantra. The restorative and clarifying effects of their meditation were extraordinary. By allowing the mind to settle, they found a greater ability to stay in the moment. And staying in the moment kept them from dwelling on the past.

Aria relayed lessons she had learned from her Transantental Medantation teachers. "When you are present, the past and the future no longer have power over you. This is your way to freedom and enlightenment."

Their medantation practice allowed Adir and Elgo to let go of criticism, complaining, fear, and resentment. Over time, it wasn't just in medantation that they let go of these burdens of the mind—they would catch themselves with a criticism, complaint, fear, or resentment coming on and simply replace it with a thought of gratitude for this moment.

By taking a pause twice per day, Adir could sense a release from the earthquake that had come to define them. Adir and Elgo embraced the solution to stay in the moment instead of reliving a painful past or fearing an uncertain future.

Stay **in the moment**

instead of reliving

a painful past or **fearing**

an uncertain future.

Soon, others in the herd noticed Adir and Elgo begin to smile as their steps became lighter, too.

Due to the three weeks of fitness, food, and med*ant*ation routines, their recovery was faster than it would have been if they simply did nothing but attempt to rest. Actively taking care of themselves added rocket fuel to recovery, taking them to new heights of mental, physical, and emotional well-being.

The work they put in self-care plus being present paid off as they were able to cast off their addiction to struggling. Without the weight of self-imposed negativity, they both felt the freedom to move forward with clarity and creativity. They were unburdened by their past as a new world awaited them.

Aria leaned up against a twig. Something clicked inside her brain and she stared straight at Adir.

He knew she was staring at him before he glanced up and met her gaze.

"Your three weeks are up," Aria said with purpose.

Adir nodded. "Thanks to you. I was thinking—"

"And your colony would be thrilled to reunite with you," she said, not finished with what she had to say. "You are in a good place, but the wrong place. You are not where you are meant to be, are you?" She leaned away from the twig.

"I . . ." Adir paused and looked sideways at Elgo. "We are . . ." Adir searched for the right words. "Yes, we are meant to be with our colony. Our family. We were born into a family, plus we have come into a family here with you . . ."

"But you are meant to be with your first family. Family is worth fighting for. Once you find it, you fight for it," said Aria as her elephant, Ella, nodded.

Her words hung in the air as a banner of truth.

"You're right! Aria, you are right!" Adir looked around. Looked at Aria and back to Ella. "It's time. We need to find our colony."

Elgo, recognizing Adir's decisive nature, looked over at Ella and thought, "Looks like we're leaving. But man, am I going to miss those eyelashes." Ella, knowing what he was thinking, blinked and grinned.

Aria and Adir looked at their elephants, then back up at each other and smiled, too.

"Will you wait until morning? That way we can give you a send-off tonight and celebrate our friendship."

So that's exactly what they did.

The evening celebration was full of laughter and joy. There were no stories of tests or troubles, only chances to revel in the now. The night ended with a toast.

"To Brio. His friendship . . . Our friendship. It is one that feels like family," said Adir, raising his glass to all the herd. "And that is the greatest gift of all."

ADIR'S NOTES TO SELF

- A good idea won't go away.
- Time is the blessing and the curse. Embrace the blessing and let go of the curse by taking the next step.
- Stop telling my earthquake story! I'm allowing it to stay in my head rent-free.
- Don't allow dis-ease to take hold. The mind and body are connected. After a personal earthquake, emotional, mental, and physical disease must not be allowed to manifest over time.
- To change my results, first change my beliefs.
- Stay in the moment instead of reliving a painful past or fearing an uncertain future.

Wrath from Land and Sky

A dir and Elgo awoke before dawn. They couldn't top their goodbyes from the previous night, so they quietly slipped out of the camp.

Ten feet into their journey, Aria and Ella emerged from the side of the trail. Ella lifted bags of fresh fruit and extended her trunk.

"Gentlemen," whispered Aria, "you are not alone. You remain in our hearts with the hope we will meet again and toast to our friendship and family." There was a pause, then Aria burst out, "But I have to ask. What exactly is your plan?"

"Plan?" mused Adir. "We were actually hoping that the plan would occur to us along the way. I kind of like John Lennant's

quote, '*Life is what happens to you when you're making other plans.*'"*
Elgo chuckled. "We figured we would skip any specific plans, head in the general direction of where we think our colony is, and be open to what life has in store for us. I believe that we will be reunited with our family soon."

"Sounds like a plan. Kind of. Sort of," said Aria with a smile and a nod. But then she froze. She locked eyes with Adir and looked like she was about to say something before just nodding again. Adir felt like he should say something, but Elgo started to walk.

With gratitude and a smile, Elgo placed the fruit over his flank and headed eastward along the banks of the Black Rock River. Adir looked back and waved one last time. This goodbye felt different than any other, but their path of self-discovery and solutions lay in front of them.

Hours passed and the trail gradually invited them downhill. By the end of the day, high clouds replaced the sun. The temperature dropped and they made camp in a clearing with modest cover. The next day, the grey sky persisted as they conversed about their will to win.

"Willpower with acceptance, drive to win with the joy of the moment, and sheer determination with absolutely letting go. We're a walking contradiction," said Adir with a chuckle. "I have

---

* He performed with a beetle named George, a walrus named Paul, and a starfish named Ringo. "Coo coo ca choo," he sang with his band on the back of an elephant.

to say it feels better to be aligned, with neither of us trying to dominate. There's a certain flow to this. I know you can feel it. Let's Stay Curious with as many options as we can find along the way. Let's see which 'good idea' won't go away. Let's test out solutions and Take Action whenever possible," said Adir to keep their spirits high.

They felt strong, both mentally and physically. With each sure step, they felt more fulfilled than they'd felt in years.

The path narrowed into a trail until eventually their only way forward was via loose rock bordered by cracks in the ground. The landscape reminded them of the fissures they'd nearly drowned in at Splitnit River. And then, as they descended, they heard the roar of a waterfall. It roared and reverberated off the rock walls all around them.

Minutes later, they gingerly peeked over the edge to find a waterfall that would not have made it on any postcard. This one was a violent cascade of water that crashed, bashed, and careened off a chaotic outcropping of steep spires, ledges, and jagged boulders.

They looked up. Pitch-black clouds were rolling in on them from the west. Lightning darted the entire breadth of the storm from north to south and back again. Bolts flashed brighter when they hit the earth. The breathtaking power of the storm made them pause. They could also see sheets of rain making a broad curtain of dark-grey streams giving in to the pull of Earth's gravity.

They were about to get pummeled by an epic storm.

Not wanting to be anywhere near the edge of a cliff when the storm hit motivated them to swivel 180 degrees and scurry back up the slope. They were forced to walk the wide expanse between two vast crevasses before they were able to turn south and walk out of the clearing toward a precipitous but promising passage. As they approached the south edge of the high clearing, Elgo shrieked in a guttural pitch.

"I see them, too," cried Adir.

Off in the distance, outpacing the storm, were three vultures headed straight toward them. When Adir and Elgo turned to head into the forest, hoping they could get away undetected, they saw three wolves stalking from the base of the trees.

They quickly turned and ran uphill along the border of the clearing.

CRACK! BOOM!

Another lightning strike overhead followed by a rumble rolling up and down the valley.

Splat. Splat. SplatSplatSplat, whoosh.

Heavy raindrops turned into a pouring, almost deafening rain. With wind suddenly blasting up the cliff and the persistent rumble of the waterfall, their eardrums felt assaulted while their adrenaline surged. Elgo slipped and stumbled onto one knee.

"The forest," yelled Adir.

Their plan to escape into the forest via a higher entry point was blocked by three more wolves flanking them. They looked back to see three additional vultures approaching from the other escape route.

Despite the rain, their feet kept moving uphill. A small squadron of vultures led by Valafar flew over a pincer formation of wolves, led by Chromia, running down the slope. Even from a distance, and through the downpour, Adir and Elgo could see her mismatched eyes were bloodred. Her pronounced fangs were savage and bloodthirsty.

Just then, a vulture from behind swooped down. With her pointed claws, she snatched Adir by the shoulders. Five more birds attacked Elgo's head and neck, slashing gashes behind his ears. The vultures, seeing vulnerable spots on Elgo's thick elephant skin, tore at the wounds to cause more pain.

Adir slipped out of the grasp of the vulture and fell to the ground. In a fluid motion of his trunk, Elgo scooped him up, deposited the ant behind his ear, then lashed ferociously overhead, hitting three vultures out of the sky with blunt, fatal force.

Valafar could sense what was next. He looked over and threw himself in front of his fellow vulture as Elgo wildly swung back to the right. Valafar took the direct hit, allowing the other vulture to retreat. Valafar spun into the splayed and brittle roots that fanned out from a downed tree. He landed there in the intense rain, broken and unconscious.

As he took a step back, Elgo's back foot descended into nothingness. Together, elephant and ant fell backward with a sloppy splash.

It was a pit left by a root ball from a fallen three-hundred-year-old oak tree. The gigantic hole was filled with rainwater flowing from the downslope—and it was large enough to trap an elephant.

More than a dozen wolves surrounded the panicked pair.

Chromia and Valafar's plan to trap them had worked.

Adir and Elgo knew they had reached the end. They bristled, prepared to die fighting.

One wolf clamped down hard on Elgo's tail. Another tore into Elgo's bloody left ear while a third, fourth, and fifth wolf took turns attacking his right ear. Wolves sunk their teeth into his hindquarters as the vultures hovered, knowing their turn would come. Death's door had opened wide.

Then the ground started to tremble. Another earthquake. How could this be? Twice in a lifetime?

Elgo's body went limp. Adir looked to the heavens, much as he had done after the earthquake in the Oasis, crying out, "Why is this happening?"

But instead of the vultures looking down, waiting to pounce, they were all looking west.

It was not an earthquake.

A stampede of elephants, with their ants perched on their heads like tiny gladiators, charged toward them. Leading the charge was Aria and her partner, Ella. The shaking ground grew in intensity as the herd closed in, the earth no match for the pounding of hundreds of thousands of pounds of warrior elephants.

Ella plowed square into Chromia's scarred fur. Chromia rolled but regained her footing right before Ella plowed into her again. Ella smashed Chromia, again and again.

Chromia bit into Ella's trunk, but Ella picked up Chromia and slammed her down against a sharp rock. Her back was broken and her rear legs flopped and contorted, but she still tried to attack Ella.

Ella and Aria dismissed Chromia, turning to see who would be their next combatant. Chromia, persistent as ever, did not let go of the fight. She bit hard on Ella's exposed Achilles' tendon. Ella whipped around, trying to slam Chromia back against more rocks at the edge of the Black Rock River crevasse, but she lost her footing. Aria, Ella, and Chromia all tumbled over the sharp edge directly at the merciless rapids.

The fighting froze. Everyone was in shock.

"Look," said Adir as he saw the lifeless body of Chromia floating toward the waterfall. Chromia slipped over the edge and was pulverized by the brutal cascade.

If she wasn't dead before she went over the edge, the Black Rock waterfall ensured that she would never take another breath. In unison, the wolves descended into a frenzy of anger as they realized that Chromia was gone.

But where were Aria and Ella?

An instant later, Ella heaved her bulk above the edge, back into view.

Her reappearance triggered a melee of bloodthirsty screams and anger from the pack of wolves. The elephants responded by pounding their feet all around Adir and Elgo.

Wolves and vultures stepped up their attack on Adir and Elgo. The deluge of rain accumulated off the slope into an instant stream of muddy water channeling into the pit. Wolves darted around elephants, trying to avoid their stomping feet.

The ground shook again as the elephants' hammering caused a ripple effect under their feet. There was a grinding crack as millions of pounds of subterranean rock shifted below.

The muddy basin that encased Adir and Elgo turned into an instant, bottomless hole.

Floooosh.

The last thing any of the surrounding animals saw of Adir and Elgo was their wide, shocked eyes.

Then nothing.

Both Aria and Ella rushed to the edge. Their friends were gone.

The disappearance of Adir and Elgo drained everyone of their willingness to fight. The vultures took off in every direction—some even went to feed off Chromia in the water below. Two others awkwardly clutched Valafar's shattered body off the roots as the root ball and dead tree slipped back into the muddy basin. They flew off to find Valafar a final resting place.

The wolves, confused and uncertain without their leader, instinctively turned uphill and ran back in the direction of the Western Mountains.

The herd stood in shock. Their attempt to rescue Adir and Elgo had ended in heartbreak.

No winners.

Only a tragic end.

If their situation weren't so desperate, Adir may have enjoyed the ride. As he was still wedged behind Elgo's ear, the vortex of air, from a veritable free fall, was contorting his antennae in all directions. It's amazing how, during real-time moments of wreckage, the mind slows everything down to a consumable, conscious string of thoughts. For Elgo, his profound awareness easily adapted to the sudden plummet. For Adir's tiny mind, it was sensory overload.

They'd gone from fighting for their lives in the mouth of a muddy pit to falling into the throat of the earth—a throat that eased into a smooth, twisting waterslide.

It was in this moment, when life would surely end, that Adir flashed back to careening down the hill and broken limbs in the Oasis. He heard Brio's voice flash through his head.

"Injured? Rest."

"In a hole? Pace yourself."

"Falling? Go with it."

Eventually, though, Adir and Elgo slowed. The smooth walls of the hole gradually narrowed. Increasing friction on Elgo's girth diminished their pace from unencumbered gravity to swift deceleration. By sheer luck, with the sides continuing to narrow, while lubricated by the muddy water that fell with them, Elgo barely squeezed through the narrowest part of the funnel. It was literally only millimeters smaller than the widest part of Elgo's belly.

They got stuck very briefly and were immersed in fallen water that followed them from above. Elgo sucked in his belly. With a *ker-ploop*, they popped out of the funnel and landed on a flat ledge eight feet below with a cacophony of water splashing on and around them.

Aside from the sounds of dripping water and their breathing, they were surrounded by silence. For about two seconds.

A rumble sounded through the darkness from above as the oak tree and its tangled web of uprooted roots careened toward the opening they'd just passed through. They were certain the dead tree and its roots would crush them, so they huddled together, bracing as best they could for what was sure to be the final moment of their lives.

But the expanse of the tangled roots saved them, spreading across the opening of the narrowest part of the hole like a net, keeping the oak tree from flying through the gap and spearing them.

They looked up.

That simple shift of their weight destabilized them both. They tipped off their perch, falling backward into another free fall.

But this section of the tunnel was the opposite of the first in texture, the rough walls brutalizing every part of their bodies. Their skulls bounced from side to side.

With each blow to the head, a burst of stars and memories flashed like fireworks—specifically, back to their last fall before Brio died. Adir relived the agonizing moment when Chromia snapped her jaws shut, ending Brio's life.

Now, in this moment that Adir was sure could be nothing more than the end of his life, he heard Brio's voice.

"Don't panic. Embrace the unknown. Have faith over force."

Adir's last thought before they were hit with a blow that turned his world completely black was: "When it's dark, hope is the light."

CHAPTER 12

Resspace Gowiddit

The groggy sensation of trying to wake up after a series of concussive blows disoriented them almost as much as the sun shining directly overhead.

Everything hurt. Their heads, backs, feet, ears.

Elgo was dabbing cold water on his torn ears when Adir managed to come to. The roar of the Black Rock Falls, off to the west, was muffled. Everything seemed muted.

Adir sat up, shaking his left leg as he tilted his head to the right. Water dripped off his antennae and his hearing tuned in to the clear, crisp sounds around him.

Now he could hear clearly, but thinking clearly was another matter. It took him time to make sense of his surroundings.

Adir got up and promptly fell over. "Sheesh," he thought to himself. "Walking straight wasn't about to happen, either." He stood up again and wobbled over toward a nearby stone.

"You're going to need to splint that or you'll be turning left for weeks," said a sweet voice behind him.

Adir snapped his head around to see Aria standing in front of her elephant. Aria ran to him and held him for a long embrace. One that neither of them thought would ever happen.

"We thought we lost you! You've got one loyal elephant on your hands there," she said, nodding toward Elgo.

"So . . . do . . . you!" Adir tipped his imaginary hat to Ella. "Loyal not just to you, but to us and all your friends in the herd." Ella smiled at the compliment. "Thank you so much for rescuing us. I would have said it earlier, of course, but I was too busy being flushed through Black Rock toilet."

Ella chuckled.

"That had to be a trip like no other," hinted Aria, prodding for details on how they'd survived their improbable slide through a billion-year-old aqueduct. "What took you seconds took us four hours. It was pretty perilous, taking narrow switchbacks down the southern embankment. But it was worth it when we spotted you and Elgo floating out the base of the falls."

Suddenly panicked, and on alert, Adir coughed out the words, "What happened to the wolf pack?"

"You're safe now. When the wolves realized Chromia was dead and the vultures had abandoned them, they tucked tail and ran. I doubt they'll be returning. The Western Mountains are simply too far away to come all this way for a grocery run of elephant tartar or skinny ant bones." Aria smirked before she inquired, "Adir, you kept mumbling something in your delirious state."

Adir sat back and started to mess with his antennae.

"You kept saying, 'Resspace gowiddit, resspace gowiddit, resspace gowiddit.' What on this green earth is resspace gowiddit?" she asked.

It took Adir a second to interpret her words. "Ahhhh," he blurted out as his fractured antennae flopped into his eyeball. "Rest. Pace. Go with it. It's what I learned in the Oasis. After a nasty fall, Brio gave us that advice. I heard it at the time but didn't truly learn it. You may find this hard to believe, but I tend to learn things the hard way."

Elgo heard this and spurted water from his trunk, blasting Adir backward. Aria chuckled as Adir shook off the well-deserved dousing.

"Brio said that when disaster strikes, our character instincts can close us off from a solution. We can stubbornly get in our own way. When we're injured, we push through. When we're in a hole, we force it or rush it. When we fall, we fight it or just plain panic.

"When the earthquake happened, I did it all. Fought. Pushed. Forced. Rushed and panicked. Everything except resspace and gowiddit."

Aria laughed.

"Did I learn my lesson after landing on my keester in the Oasis? Nope.

"Did I learn to pace myself in the Mudflats? Not even a little.

"Did I give us time to think things through in the Maswali Forest? Nope. I rushed us through the magnificent baobabs. I barely looked up to take it in.

"Did I prepare at all before launching directly into the deadly Potea Desert? Shoot no. I virtually forced Elgo to march into certain death.

"Did I help Brio in our escape from the vultures and wolves? I wish. Instead, I panicked.

"Did my time spent on self-care and being present make a dent in my stubborn self? Maybe a little. Maybe it primed the pump of self-discovery!

"It wasn't until our fall down the Black Rock hole that I truly stopped fighting.

"This long, post-earthquake fall has been a hell of a lesson.

"Brio said, 'Have faith over force.' But the only thing I've had faith in is myself—and not even the larger self that includes

Elgo! I kept thinking I'm alone in this. That my way is the right way. That I could use my willpower to get through it—I just had to keep trying. But how could I ever embrace the necessity of alignment with Elgo when I've ignored the most important thing of all?"

"What do you mean?" asked Aria.

"I'm talking about how my strength is *holding on* and Elgo's strength is his *letting go.* We felt this on the trail after we left you and the herd. We joked about being a walking contradiction. But we loved the feeling of synergy and alignment.

"I needed to have faith without forcing things, to have faith that the journey will lead us to where we need to be. To detach from preconceptions. Just rest with the intention, pace, and go with it."

Have **faith** you will journey
to the place you need to be.

Aria let Adir's revelation suspend in the air before saying, "I have a gift for you. Our oxpecker guests found this at the White Rock Creek crossing." Aria went to a nearby rock and pulled out a shiny, resin-coated six-petal plumeria flower with words that were immediately familiar to Adir.

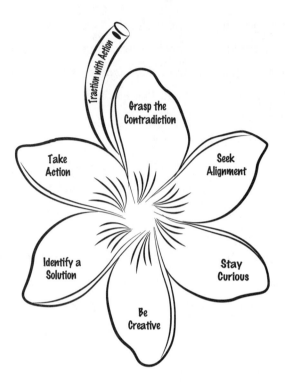

"How the . . . ?" said Adir, holding the treasured item from Brio.

"This is it. Here, look," Adir said, thinking out loud. "The solution between us is trust. Because actionable solutions lie in faith, not force. Neither of us is more important than the other.

"There is a way to take safe and measured risks—to both grow and simplify at the same time. If we don't force a direction, we can just enjoy the journey."

Faith over force.

Adir turned his head and his antennae flopped straight at Aria and Ella.

He paused, then blurted out, "Hey. I've been thinking . . . How would you and Ella like to continue? You know—continue, you know, down the path with Elgo and, uh, me?"

Aria smiled. Ella blinked her gorgeous eyelashes. Elgo, sitting in the middle of the pond, froze, a half-chewed pond weed sticking out the corner of his mouth.

Elgo's eyes darted from Ella, to Adir, to Aria, who said, "But . . . we're so different, you and I. Opposites, really. You could say . . . 'a contradiction.'"

She paused again.

"That sounds like an alignment we could all be curious about," she said, looking at Elgo.

"Tell you what. Let's spend enough time to *resspace*," she said, taking his hand, "and we'll talk about it."

"Deal. Let's *gowiddit*," said Adir, beaming from antennae to flagged antennae.

ADIR'S NOTES TO SELF

- Have faith you will journey to the place you need to be.
- Faith over force.
- Enjoy the journey. Stay present in the activity.
- Let go of the future. It hasn't happened yet.

CHAPTER 13

When Action Gets Traction

They stayed near the river's bank for a while.

The base of the falls was simultaneously new and also deeply familiar. Adir eased into a more forgiving mindset with the support of his silent elephant. They were both a cactus and a vine, completely in harmony and aligned. He delved into his inner journey, comforted by the knowledge that there would be time for an outer journey. *Letting go* didn't mean they were lazy or motionless. They didn't have to change their personality; they just paced themselves in a conscious, trusting way.

Elgo was more injured than he let on. His physical and emotional maladies mended slowly. Eventually, he stopped feeling like he had to stay stuck to feel at home. It was as if chains were broken on his limiting beliefs and he brought back a technique he'd learned on the path to the Oasis. With Adir's help, every time they started thinking about something negative, they'd have their *Pattern Buster* conversation.

For example, when they imagined forcing a result, like a Mansion by the Ocean, Adir would say, "Thank you for that thought, Elgo. But let's get back to our intention. Our intention is to enjoy the journey. Let's *gowiddit*."

When you **fixate** on a **result**,

remind yourself to

enjoy the journey.

Adir and Elgo would revel in the sweet feeling as they imagined the journey before them. If they found themselves pushing or forcing an idea, they would interrupt this familiar pattern by replacing it with an elephant buzz. They fully imagined how they were completely aligned with that delicious moment when they would reunite with their colony. They drew from the Gold Dot technique of infusing all five senses coupled with the emotion that elicited an elephant buzz. They imagined, in full detail, what their future would look like, smell like, taste like, feel like, and sound like. Then they'd add the emotions of satisfaction, gratitude, and joy to flesh out the picture. Each time, this routine ended in a deep breath and a knowing sigh.

Two weeks passed. The trauma from the Black Rock battle lost its physical and psychological aftershocks and their bodies proved to be a renewable resource as the charge surrounding the battle and the earthquake fizzled into a distant memory. They banned stories of loss, despair, or frustration. If they had any fears of anything, they acknowledged them, but then relegated them to "But that's not now." Pattern busting became a normal part of every moment of every day.

"You know what I'd like right now?" said Adir.

"A picnic?" said Aria.

"Ah yes, we ants love picnics. So, in addition to a picnic," said Adir, marveling at Aria's delicious sense of humor, "what I'd like is to introduce you to my colony. They must be ahead somewhere. Aren't you curious?"

"That would be better than a picnic!" said Aria. "Can we go now, or do we have to keep talking about it?" she asked, spurring Adir on.

A little later, in the midst of a quiet moment beside the river, Aria and Ella went over to the rest of her herd. They all already knew about Aria and Ella's growing relationship with Adir and Elgo, so no one was caught by surprise when Aria announced that they were going with Adir and Elgo. The herd simply felt joy that Aria and Ella were happy, while sad that they may never see them again.

The very next day, after a few trumpeted "Yahoos!" the herd bid the foursome their final farewells.

"Let's go," said Aria. And with that, they were off, following the even ground on the north side of Black Rock River.

"Yes, let's go," pronounced Adir, tilting his head, his still floppy antenna not yet fully healed, to point out their course downstream.

Two days into the trek, they noticed birds in the sky. Some were flying up, riding a thermal. Others were flying down in a line. Others were flying in all directions. What lay ahead was clearly a happening location for birds of all kinds.

As they got closer, across the river, a modest sign had the words *Birds of a Feather Hospital*.

"Hospital? I'm sure a bird doctor can fix a left-leaning ant," said Aria with a smile. "Let's get that antenna of yours fixed up, Adir."

"Which antenna?" he joked as the broken one continuously whacked his eyes every time Elgo took a step.

After registering and waiting in the waiting room, they heard, "Adir?" from the front desk. Adir and Aria walked down the hall.

Within minutes they were headed back outside with a splint of freshwater reeds on either side of Adir's injured antenna.

"Who's hungry?" said Adir to the two elephants who were surrounded by a room full of shocked birds. "There's a cafeteria down the hall. Let's grab some chow," he added as he walked in a straight line for the first time in weeks.

When they entered the massive space, it was noisy and full of life. After being seated and served, Ella froze. Her eyes were wide and locked on something across the dining hall. Elgo looked over at her, then in the direction of two larger birds playing checkers along the far wall. One was black—a vulture. The other was a brown owl in a neck brace.

It was no ordinary owl.

It was Brio.

Brio?

BRIO!

And across from him was Valafar in a wing-sling.

Valafar? And Brio?

Mid-chew, Adir and Aria looked up at their pachyderm pals, then arched their necks to see what was so shocking.

What followed was absolute mayhem. Feathers flew. Cafeteria trays flipped by the dozens into bona fide pandemonium. Adir and Elgo led the charge toward the unsuspecting Brio and Valafar.

The reunion was epic and wonderful, though, eventually, they had to apologize to the onlookers for the disturbance they'd caused, set things right as best they could, and hoof it back across the river where there was space to reunite.*

---

* With a healthy serving of "catch up."

Brio and Valafar didn't leave each other's side. Both were on crutches and moved slowly but surely over to a log where they sat gingerly.* The kings of contradiction indeed.

"Your neck?" Adir was flabbergasted. "How?"

"Ah, this old thing? When you can spin your head 135 degrees in either direction, you get a pretty flexible connection between this good-looking face and this hot body," said Brio, accentuating his words with wing tips that brushed over his torso.

"You two are . . . ?" added Aria.

"Buddies, now," rasped Valafar. "You know, I can't quite remember why I didn't like Brio. Could have been that his nocturnal ways oppose my diurnal routines. Maybe it was jealousy about his way of finding fresh snacks and not having to pick over dead meat. Shoot. I don't even know. We talked about our differences—"

"Your living, breathing, everything-about-you contradictions," corrected Adir.

"Exactly. Could two birds be more different? But, truth be told, we have more in common than either of us realized." He pointed his crutch at the sign across the river. "Birds of a feather . . ."

—————————

* The next time you see an alligator and a chicken playing tag, or a lit candle and a pail of water square dancing, think of Brio and Valafar enjoying each other's company.

". . . flock together," said Aria, finishing off the cliché.

Brio jumped into the conversation again. "It was more than just being birds. We were stuck in beds next to each other and it forced us to talk. In real life, with all the chaos of chasing and running away, it never occurred to us to just talk. More important than just speaking, we listened. We each actively listened to the other. We consciously set aside our biases. We stopped the habit of tuning out the other animal while planning what we want to say next. We knew we have conflicting views, but for the first time, we took the time to truly hear the other side. This is the beauty of achieving alignment by grasping contradiction as the first step of the Solution Loop.

"What if we had stopped the pattern of trying to be right all the time and dedicated that time to letting go instead? Sure, we are birds of a feather, but we are also creatures of habit. My habits were 'right' to me. Valafar's habits were 'right' to him. Without us taking the time to talk, to align, to be curious and creative, we would never find the beauty of connection over differences."

"But how did you end up here?" interrupted Adir. "You were *dead* the last time we saw you—both of you were!"

Valafar jumped in. "Loyalty is a big thing with us vultures. My guys brought me straight here. Turns out the oxpeckers love gossip, so the bird hospital caught wind of Brio's tangle with Chromia. An emergency AmbuCrane found him and picked him up. So here we are."

Getting back to the main point and the lesson he wanted to convey, Brio continued. "We had every reason to dislike each other. Valafar went after my buddies."

"He ate all his food and left no scraps for us," Valafar edged in with a lighthearted tone. "The list goes on."

"We met in the hospital," Brio said next. "I was in the hospital on a very slow, long mend. I couldn't move. Stuck in bed. A long while later, who do they put with me in my hospital room? This handsome devil."

"Devil?"

"You ain't no angel," quipped Brio.

"True. How about friend?"

"They wheeled in this handsome *friend* three feet from my bed. He's out cold. He wakes up."

"Couldn't move!" said Valafar, itching to tell his side of the story. "I wake up and look over and see the last bird I ever wanted to see alive."

"Whaaaaa?" breathed Aria and Adir alongside Ella and Elgo.

"Truth is, we got to talking. Man, that owl can talk," Valafar said with a raspy lilt as the audience of four raised eyebrows and nodded in agreement.

The foursome looked from Valafar to Brio and back again as they tried to digest the improbability of this bizarre turn of events.

"Fact is," added Brio, relishing in his newfound friendship and this reunion with his mentees, "we both decided something very important in today's world."

"What's that?" asked Adir.

"In a relationship, ANY relationship, as soon as you choose a side, you become part of the problem."

When you choose a side, you become part of the problem.

Those words suspended in the air like a banner of ultimate truth.

"When you choose your side," said Aria, testing the concept in her own heart, "you become part of the problem?" She paused for a moment, then her eyes got wide. "Yes. Yes, that's it! When I choose my side . . ."

"When I choose my side, when you choose your side," said Adir to Elgo and back to the odd pairing of birds, "we become part of the problem."

ADIR'S NOTES TO SELF

- Even once you've chosen a goal, remind yourself to enjoy the journey.
- When I choose my side, I become part of the problem.

CHAPTER 14

From Darkness to Light

Brio and Valafar were inseparable. They took turns riding on the backs of either Elgo or Ella. Valafar preferred Ella because, in his words, "She smells better."*

To pass the time while riding on the backs of their elephants and marching up the trail, Adir and Aria decided to replicate the six-petal plumeria as a motivational keepsake that they could share with others. They reasoned that if they got value out of following the Solution Loop, others would, too.

---

* Seeing that Valafar had no feathers on his head and neck because he buried himself into the flesh of rotting carcasses, Brio didn't quite know if the vulture was an authority on what smells good.

At one of their stops, they shared the Solution Loop trinket with a few creatures. One said, "If I could have ten more, I'll give you this bunch of bananas."

Adir and Aria looked at Brio. He nodded his approval. "Deal," Aria replied as Adir gathered up ten Solution Loop plumerias from their inventory.

At their next stop, others traded fresh blueberries for their remaining inventory.

Adir turned to Brio and Valafar. "Well, I'll be jitterbugged. Sold out. We made these Solution Loop reminders for fun and now we have a business all of a sudden. Folks seem to like a keep-sake for keeping themselves unstuck."

Holding a replica of the Solution Loop plumeria, Adir glanced over at a Gold Dot that landed on the crown of Elgo's head. Brio tracked his gaze and posed a question: "Do you remember when I said, *True acceptance is the beginning of your new Gold Dot?*" Elgo and Adir nodded. "My friends, I also added, *Keep pursuing profound acceptance. When you can sit with the memory of your earthquake, and there is no charge, no negative buzz, you will finally be able to reinvent.*"

"Ah yes. I was thinking something along the same lines," said Adir, carrying on the thought. "There's zero charge around the memory of the earthquake." Adir walked over toward Aria in the resting spot they occupied for the moment. "Thanks to Aria, I consciously stopped bringing it up. This stopped me, and especially Elgo, from reliving it. Now? I can say 'earthquake' all I want—earthquake . . . earthquake . . . earthquake—and I feel nothing."

Brio and Valafar smiled as Adir continued.

"You know, I became really attached to the idea of a Mansion by the Ocean. The whole five-sensory scene that I told you about earlier, Brio—with warmth of the sunshine washing over me, my body healthy and fit, my home paid in full. No debt. I used to think about the smells of the ocean and the vibrant green trees all around, plus the creek I could hear off to my right.

"The feeling of gratitude, satisfaction, and joy were all part of this experience of the Mansion by the Ocean. As I would stand on the balcony with my wife, she has her top right hand on my left shoulder. The sounds of the surf and our kids playing near the waves . . ."

"Wife? Kids? Tap the brakes there, Lover Boy," said Aria.

"Right. Well, I've been thinking I don't need to get ahead of myself," said Adir.

"Exactly," said Brio.

"But . . . there's no harm in thinking ahead," said Aria, "especially when the heart does the thinking." This let Adir know she actually liked the idea.

"Now, what about your new Gold Dot?" Brio reminded them, tilting his head toward the Gold Dot.

"Right. I'm thinking I need to set my intention out there but focus on a Gold Dot that is more immediately attainable."

"Like what?"

"What if my Gold Dot goals are lined up with our little six-petal plumeria business? Each time I see a Gold Dot, I'll say to myself, *I'm grateful for four new customers every day.*"

"I like it," said Aria.

Both Elgo and Ella had perceptible elephant buzzes.

"They like it, too," said Valafar as he felt the shudder of delight under his talons.

"The mansion may come; it may not. But I'll enjoy each day. No more of this *I'll be happy when . . .* mindset. I'll take happy now. Even better," added Adir, "I'll take fulfilled now. What could be better than that?"

This got Brio's attention. "Fulfilled is fully developing one's abilities and character. I like that, Adir. You have become a student developing in the intersection of mastery and growth."

Adir smiled and effortlessly reached out to hold Aria's hand.

Adir gathered Gold Dots and put them all over the place. The sight of them reminded him that he simply wanted four sales each day, every day. Some days their sales fell short of their goal. Some days they sold out of every last flower trinket. Either way, he knew his efforts were making a difference in the lives of others.

Most important to Adir and Elgo, they were happy, and fulfilled, with every passing moment.

At one point, he was talking to a customer who told him that an Oasis colony of ants, who had lost their home and loved ones in an earthquake, would likely want some of the Solution Loop plumerias, too.

"Colony? Where?" demanded Adir out of excitement.

"One town over," said the customer, pointing downstream, while not realizing the significance of this news. "You just—" he said, without having the chance to finish his sentence.

Adir dumped the purchased inventory on the customer's lap, torqued his body, and dashed directly to Elgo and his friends.

"This way, boys and girls. We've got a family to see!"

Adir reached up and pulled off the splint. It was due to come off anyway. He loved the feeling of fresh air wafting past the tiny sensilla hairs on his newly mended antenna. Excitement and anticipation emanated from his heart and lungs.

By afternoon they rounded the corner of the town and— there they were. Their long-lost colony. Adir and Elgo charged straight, carefully, into the middle of the throng. Others gathered around. Little ones ran off to alert other members of the colony. It was another joyous reunion just a couple of months after finding Brio alive in the hospital.

Adir hugged every member of his colony. Dozens of family members surrounded one of Elgo's legs to give him a group hug. While mixing and mingling, Aria and Ella had to endure the nudge, nudge, wink, wink teasing from all of Adir's cousins as they realized they would eventually become cousins-in-law.

The reunion party lasted all night. It was nearly dawn before animals began slipping off to bed. Brio and Valafar were passed out in identical Lazy-Bird Chairs, legs kicked up, mouths open, snoring in concert. By first light, the only four left were Aria, Ella, Elgo, and Adir.

Full sunrise was a half hour away. In the meantime, the four travelers wandered up to Town Ridge. They chose a spot and looked out to what may be their future Oasis.

Or maybe their future was right here.

Aria rested her head on Adir's shoulder. Underneath them were Ella and Elgo resting their heads and sides against each other.

Birds in the valley roused, as they were wont to do this time of day. The sky went from pitch black above to a slow, semicircular spread that began with purple coal, then cerulean blue, burnt orange to blanch yellow. The brightest bend of golden light divulged where the sun would peek above the horizon.

As the first flare of the sun crested, Adir said to the sun, "Look at you . . ."

Darkness let go of its grasp on the night.

Morning broke through with new light, promise, and hope.

Acknowledgments

On our journey together, there is no such thing as being stuck, only a setback waiting for a breakthrough. Thank you for reading this book. May it take you to an oasis of fulfillment.

To my wife and kids. Our personal earthquakes seem irrelevant when we are together. In fact, our breakthroughs have all come from the setbacks we face together. Michelle, Max, Alex, and Bella, you all are the light of hope that I can count on and cherish.

Kelsey Grode, thank you, thank you, thank you! Your expertise at the intersection of storytelling, content delivery, and the human condition was helpful beyond measure. Anyone who gets to work with you is a fortunate soul. Thank you to both Katie Dickman and Alyn Wallace for lending your editing expertise to these pages. To Matt Holt, you believed in this book the second you picked it up. Thank you for your decades of experience and insights.

Harville Hendrix, PhD. It took *your years of expertise* to distill "the 3rd Reality" into one lunch conversation. You are the inflection point at the exact right moment this book needed. Thank you. Special thanks to Helen Hunt for your love and support. Melinda Marcus, one lunch, plus your three words "and the earthquake," were the catalyst I needed to trigger this important work.

To the Stone family, particularly their patriarch and my dear friend, David. Your South Carolina oasis represents your values of serve, love, give, and enjoy. To Peter and Rita Thomas, each time I write what Brio would have said, my mind hears both of your voices. There is no greater gift you've shared in our lives than that magical combination of profound friendship and mentorship, wrapped in a profound package. Meg Kuehn, your initial "story-forward" comments on the first draft were immensely helpful. Michael and Inna O'Brian, for their friendship and relaying the lessons on radical acceptance. To Dr. Leigh Erin Connealy and Patrick McCall, thank you for leading by example. Again, another magical combo of love, companionship, and growth.

To the Veritas Forum. Through the rises, falls, climbs, interminable skids, and reinventions, the honesty and insights we share are beyond measure. Thanks to Kurt Kretsinger, Mike Schoder, Tim McDonald, Neeti Gupta, Martin Reavis, Nicole Shaw, Holly Shields, Gary Walker, Jorge Azpe, Michael Holmes, and Larry Patterson (plus your spouses, Jenny, Julia, Cynthia, et al) who contributed to this journey. To Victoria Labalme, Frank Oz, and the Eagle Nest gang, each and every one of our conversations added to the fabric of this book. In particular, Steven Pressfield's early input. Thank you.

Acknowledgments

To John David Conn and his sage father, David, for their wise counsel. Particular gratitude to early readers with their above-and-beyond insights: Tim Durkin, Shari Krueger Dunn, Bob Phillips, Erin Holm, Ken Wright, Joseph Barisonzi, Brian Kennedy, Kimberly Todd-Tullos, Kathy Middleton, Michelle A. Wilson, Bruce Benner, and Jonas Bull. A special shout-out to Dr. George Burriss—yes, my friend, faith is indeed more powerful than force.

To my brother, Steven, and sister, Christa, I love you. To my mother-in-law, LaDell Lemmons, and Texas family, with open arms and loving ways, you took me in as your own. Let me save the most significant expression of gratitude for last. My mom, Patricia. Your fingerprints, or rather, your "heart-prints," are all over this book. I love you and deeply appreciate your contributions to this story, as you live by example!

About the Author

Photo by Hal Samples

As they face a spectrum of challenges, **Vince Poscente** helps business leaders with sustainable breakthroughs. His "Do what the competition is not willing to do" approach to opportunities, obstacles, and resilience has been used by Fortune 500 companies, sales teams, and industry association meetings around the globe. In addition to being a *New York Times, #1 Wall Street Journal, #1 USA Today* bestselling author and in-demand corporate presenter, he's an Olympic competitor (Speed Skiing, Albertville, France) and Hall of Fame speaker in both Canada and the USA. *Meetings & Conventions* identified Vince as "Meeting Planners' Favorite Speaker." His **Full Speed Ahead** and **Setback to Breakthrough** conference keynotes are delivered with unforgettable energy, engaging humor, and practical takeaways. Vince has led expeditions to summit and named Himalayan mountains after everyday heroes.

About the Author

Vince lives in Dallas, Texas, with his wife, Michelle. As parents they marvel at the love and respect Max, Alexia, and Isabella have earned on their own unique paths.

For more detailed information, keynote availability, transformational learning tools, and entertaining video clips, check out @VincePoscente and www.VincePoscente.com.

VINCE•POSCENTE

Business Breakthroughs

"Do what the competition is not willing to do."

VPI is a strategic consulting and professional development firm specializing in transformations from intrinsic motivation to accelerated corporate results.

Our clients share our passion for excellence at work while having fun along the way. We have served the most respected and innovative companies around the world.

Services

Drive Sales
Enabling business leaders and sales forces to reach extraordinary goals in record time

Enhance Leadership
Equipping leaders with the breakthrough tools necessary to create a culture of engaged and eager teammates

Sustain Self-Management
Cascading our "Results Only" approach to every on-site and remote employee

Enrich Communication Skills
Ensuring each employee optimizes impact and influence both professionally and personally

To learn how Vince Poscente International can help you and your organization or to discuss speaking availability, please email us at info@vinceposcente.com.

To access free videos, breakthrough tools, and how to win in the business of life, please visit www.vinceposcente.com.

Binge on
Entertaining,
Educating,
and Motivating
Breakthrough Videos

VincePoscente.com/videos